THE STATE
AGAINST BLACKS

THE STATE AGAINST BLACKS

Walter E. Williams

PROFESSOR OF ECONOMICS
GEORGE MASON UNIVERSITY

NEW PRESS

McGRAW-HILL BOOK COMPANY

New York   St. Louis   San Francisco   Hamburg

Mexico   Toronto

A Manhattan Institute for
Policy Research Book

1 2 3 4 5 6 7 8 9 0 DOCDOC 8 7 6 5 4 3 2

ISBN 0-07-070378-7

LIBRARY OF CONGRESS CATALOGING IN PUBLICATION DATA

Williams, Walter E. (Walter Edward), 1936–
The state against Blacks.
1. Afro-Americans—Employment—Law and legisla-
tion. 2. Afro-Americans—Legal status, laws, etc.
I. Title.
KF3464.W54   344.73'016396073   82–7232
ISBN 0–07–070378–7   347.30416396073   AACR2

Book design by Christine Aulicino.

*To Mom, who kept the faith
and did it her way.*

My race needs no special defense, for the past history of them in this country proves them to be the equal of any people anywhere. All they need is an equal chance in the battle of life.

—*Robert Smalls*
Congressman, Beaufort, S.C.
1874–1886

ACKNOWLEDGMENTS

The research for this book began in 1975 when I was a National Fellow at the Hoover Institution on War, Peace and Revolution at Stanford University. Unencumbered by teaching responsibilities and surrounded by good minds that year in residence assisted me in developing my ideas.

Some years later, with the appropriate digressions, I basically completed the book with the assistance of a Rockefeller research grant and the cheerful assistance of the Heritage Foundation in Washington, D.C. The Heritage Foundation provided research assistance, materials and a place to hang my hat while I searched the Library of Congress, sometimes successfully and sometimes in vain, for information. Appreciation also goes to the Scaife Foundation in its assistance grant, which allowed me the time to put the manuscript into its final form.

To fully list scholars, mentors and colleagues who gave me useful criticism would be hopeless. Such a list would range from my tenacious mentors at UCLA to my Temple University colleague Professor Lynn Holmes, who allowed me to exploit his mind.

A final and special thanks goes to Pat Conboy, my research assistant at Temple University, and my secretary/assistant, Pamela Crawford, who cheerfully managed various stages of the manuscript.

CONTENTS

LIST OF TABLES

INTRODUCTION

A person would have to be dead or completely insensitive not to realize that for the last twenty years race has been a major focus of public debate and public policy. What is reducible to racism, bigotry and callousness on the behalf of whites is most often featured as the cause of the current condition of many blacks. The assumption is made that since blacks do not differ biologically from whites in ways that should affect socioeconomic status, the different status of blacks in the society reflects racism and mistreatment by whites. Therefore, the fight to promote equality and opportunity is portrayed as a struggle between the forces of good and the forces of evil. To the extent that the problems of blacks are cast this way, more-effective policies are ignored and people seeking to help blacks set out to find evil people and punish them.

The problems with explaining the plight of black people in terms of good and evil are: (1) that approach does not yield testable hypotheses, a basic requirement of science and (2) finding and punishing evil people cannot explain the economic progress of minorities in the United States or any place else. For example, Jews in the U.S. and elsewhere did not have to wait for the end of anti-Semitism in order to prosper as a group. Japanese-Americans did not have to wait to become liked in order to be the second highest group in the U.S. in most measures of well-being. West Indian blacks did not have to wait for racism to end to earn a median income, in the U.S., that is just slightly below that for the nation as a whole. People discriminated against elsewhere frequently exhibit similar patterns; these are briefly discussed in chapter 1.

Clearly, the experience of Orientals, Jews and West Indians calls into question the hypothesis that racial bigotry can be a complete explanation of the difficulties that blacks face in America. The point is that if racial discrimination is not the most important cause, then economic and political resources need to be reallocated to address the more important causes of the disadvantages faced by many blacks.

There was in the past gross denial of basic rights of and gross discrimination against blacks in the U.S. Residual discrimination remains. But the basic premise of this book is that racial bigotry and discrimination is neither a complete nor a satisfactory explanation for the *current* condition of many blacks in America.

We will see that instead of racial discrimination and bigotry, it is the "rules of the game" that account for many of the economic handicaps faced by blacks. The rules of the game are the many federal, state and local laws that regulate economic activity. Game rules can, and do, influence the outcome of the game. As such, there are many laws in the United States that systematically discriminate against the employment and advancement of people who are outsiders, latecomers and poor in resources. It is important to point out that these laws or rules discriminate against certain people irrespective of race. However, because of their history in the U.S., blacks are disproportionately represented in the class of people described as outsiders, latecomers and resourceless.

What all of this means is that there are significant differences in opportunities for upward mobility which blacks face relative to ethnic groups despised and disadvantaged in the past. The major difference is that when other ethnics became urbanized, markets were freer and less regulated. When blacks became urbanized and *received the franchise,* they very often found those avenues of traditional upward mobility closed through various forms of business and occupational regulation. For example (explored more fully in chapter 6), an illiterate, uneducated poor person in New York in the 1920s could get a used car and become an owner-operator of a taxi. Today a person seeking a similar route to upward mobility must pay $60,000 just for a license to do so.

If the evidence bears out the argument that there are laws that eliminate economic opportunities, then political resources should be expended in the direction of modifying those laws. The government, at various levels, can exert its authority to ensure that all people have unrestricted access to legitimate markets.

The plan of this book will be that of examining several specific market restrictions. However, in order to demystify various aspects of race, the early chapters will investigate propositions, axioms and definitions that have clouded our understanding of one of America's most complex problems.

THE STATE
AGAINST BLACKS

CHAPTER 1

Discrimination Axioms and Discrimination Facts

As for doing good, that is one of the professions
which are full.
—Henry David Thoreau
 Walden, I, Economy

BLACKS, BY EVERY MEASURE of group well-being, experience a lower standard of living than Americans in general. Blacks compared with whites suffer lower income, educational achievement, occupational status and life expectancy and experience less employment stability.[1] The most frequently cited causes of group differences between blacks and whites are racial discrimination in employment, schooling, housing and law enforcement, plus that catch-all "institutional racism."

Racial discrimination having been identified as the prime cause of black disadvantage, several propositions are seen to characterize the racial literature. They are:

a. Without economic advances, political gains will be limited, and vice versa.[2]

b. Homogeneous association based on race impedes the economic progress of minorities because: (1) it leads to a "distorted" distribution of public goods; (2) it denies minorities many job opportunities, and (3) it denies individuals the "beneficial" results from interacting with individuals of different backgrounds and cultural values.[3]

c. No attempts to provide equal opportunities in our society, or to improve conditions among deprived groups,
are likely to succeed unless we eliminate *or* counteract
racism.[4]

d. . . . one effective way to build up capabilities quickly
among the most deprived members of the black population, and to enhance the self-respect of the already capable members, is for Negroes to dominate most public and
private activities in predominately Negro neighborhoods.[5]

e. . . . greater progress can be made by eliminating discrimination in employment. For it is there that the most important barriers to equality of opportunity are found. Far
more than is now being done can be accomplished by
extension of equal opportunity, affirmative action, and related employment programs. . . . The basic concept is
that blacks and other minorities be hired at all skill levels
in approximately the same proportion that they bear to
the total labor force in the locality. This approach could
well be extended by law to all private employers, not just
government contractors. . . . In this way, the opportunity
system could move well beyond equal opportunity toward
positive action that actively seeks out blacks and other
minorities.[6]

Throughout these propositions, and many others in the
discussion of race, runs the common theme: There are collective forces that seek to deny blacks socioeconomic opportunity which must be offset by some other force in order
to give blacks equal chances. It is this general intellectual
thrust that will be challenged throughout this book. Does
group socioeconomic progress depend upon whether the
general society likes or dislikes the group in question?

Racial Conflict

Racial antagonism in the United States, from subtle innuen-
does to open conflict, is a widely known phenomenon. Racial,
as well as religious, conflict has existed in the United States
since the founding of our country. The Irish, Italian, Negro,
Jew, Puerto Rican, Polish, Chinese, Japanese, Swedish and
most other ethnic groups have commonly shared the experi-

ence of being discriminated against in one form or another.[7] The extent of discrimination faced by these groups has differed in degree and kind. Similarly, the response to discrimination by these ethnic groups has varied between groups and within groups. In all ethnic groups, members divide on the issue of cultural pluralism versus assimilation.

As highly publicized as racial conflict is in the United States, what seems not to be appreciated, to any significant degree, is that racial conflict is a phenomenon that is unique neither to the United States nor to the twentieth century. Racial preferences, grouping and conflict are a permanent global feature of man's history.

In England there is wide discrimination against West Indians, Pakistanis and Indians.[8] In South Africa there is the widely known societal bifurcation and hostility between white, Asian, colored and black Africans. Contrary to what modern day rhetoric would have us believe, racial oppression and discrimination find no color group innocent of their practice. Colored peoples racially discriminate against whites as well as other colored peoples. For example, in Africa, black Africans often discriminate against Arabs, Syrians, Lebanese, Indians and Chinese.[9] In recent history there has been expulsion *en masse* of some 50,000 Asians from Uganda.[10] There have also been massive expulsions of Asians from Kenya.[11] Although the situation is nowhere nearly as extreme as in Uganda and Kenya, Asians encounter racial discrimination and hostility in the other countries of East Africa and Central Africa, Tanganyika, Zambia and Malawi.[12]

In addition to racial discrimination and conflict between peoples of different racial stock, there is discrimination and conflict between people of identical racial stock but of different "tribes" and/or religious groups. Widely known examples of these types of conflicts are Irish Catholics versus Irish protestants; Ebos of Biafra versus the Hausa of Nigeria; Watusi versus Bantu; strife between the Kikuyu and the Luo in Kenya; and the periodic massacres of the Batutsi and the Bahutu in Rwanda and Burundi.[13]

Lesser-known examples of ethnic conflict are those

found in Lebanon, with the Muslims versus Christians; Belgium, with the Flemings versus the Walloons; Ceylon, with the Singhalese versus the Tamil; and in Canada, with English-speaking versus French-speaking populations.

Chinese in Southeast Asia

In most of the countries of southeast Asia, the minority Chinese population suffers the status of the most despised minority.[14] The Chinese have always constituted a small minority—no more than 10 percent of the entire southeast Asian population—and numbering less than 3 percent in such countries as Indonesia and the Philippines. The hostility of the indigenous population toward the Chinese has been manifested by frequent massacres and occasional deportation of segments of the Chinese population.[15]

No less prevalent than the hostile racial climate the Chinese face in southeast Asia is their considerable economic strength; in Indonesia, as we have noted, the Chinese constitute less than *3 percent* of the entire population. Through their roles as middlemen, merchants and money handlers, Chinese produce 30 to 40 percent of the national product.[16] The disproportionate Chinese economic power can be seen in most other countries of southeast Asia—in the Philippines, Malaysia[17] and Thailand,[18] for example. In Malaysia the Chinese constitute a larger percentage of the population (37 percent), but they produce 60 percent of the national income.

From time to time, numerous measures have been undertaken to restrict the economic power held by the Chinese segment of the southeastern Asia population. These measures have ranged from outright expropriation of property and job reservation laws to harsh business licensing requirements.[19] Despite measures to restrict Chinese enterprise, the Chinese population clearly enjoys a higher standard of living. Moreover, there is wholesale evasion and corruption of these anti-Chinese discriminatory laws. In many enterprises reserved for the indigenous population, what appears to be indigenous ownership and control is really a front or a dummy for a Chinese owner. Such illegalities are often effected with the connivance and the participation of officials who are charged with the enforcement of the discriminatory laws.

Racial Malevolence and Economic Progress

No attempt is being made here to fully examine racial hostility. We only want to establish its widespread existence. Chinese, Indians and Jews, as despised aliens, have enjoyed economic progress in a racially hostile environment. A fuller examination would suggest that the same is true about Armenians, Greeks and Jews in the successor states of the Ottoman Empire. The fact that despised minorities sometimes make significant economic gains throws into question at least two axiomatic statements made in the literature on race. First, benevolence on the behalf of the larger society is neither a necessary nor a sufficient condition for an ethnic minority to achieve economic power.[20] Second, economic power can exist in the absence of what is traditionally considered political power.[21]

Obviously, if the dominant racial group expropriates all the wealth of the nonpreferred group, such as in the extreme case of slavery, little or no economic progress can take place. But under less extreme cases, the effect of racial hostility on group progress is less clear. The point is not one of justifying racial malevolence; nor is it one of saying that racial malevolence is of no consequence.

Racial benevolence is one part of racial rhetoric; political power is another. The cases of the Chinese in southeast Asia, Indians in Africa, and Armenians in the post-Ottoman Empire suggest that political power is not a necessary condition for group economic progress. In our own country, we have seen how Jews have prospered in the face of hostility and discrimination. Although Jews have significant political power *now,* their strongest socioeconomic progress occurred at a time when they were politically unimportant even in areas where they were most highly concentrated.[22]

Japanese-Americans have always been and are now politically insignificant. On the West Coast they were subjected to some of the harshest forms of persecution. The Oriental Exclusion Act of 1882 proscribed citizenship. This set the Japanese up for being denied land ownership. California, in 1913, enacted an anti-Japanese land law. Under its terms, a person ineligible for citizenship could not own agricultural land or lease it for more than three years. Over the ensuing years, ten other western states adopted the California policy. The U.S. Supreme Court upheld the constitutionality of these state laws.[23] Eventually Japanese were interned during World War II and their property was virtually confiscated.

Without a doubt Japanese (and Chinese) have had experiences which, at least according to prevailing thought, make them prime candidates for group disadvantage. Yet by almost any measure selected, they are one of the most "successful" ethnic groups in America. To cite some 1975 figures on socioeconomic characteristics of the Japanese-American: 19.5 percent of employed Japanese were professional workers compared to 15.6 percent of white workers (that of the Chinese was 25 percent); unemployment rate for the Japanese was 2.4 percent while that of whites was 4.1 percent; similarly in labor force participation and education the Japanese and the Chinese exceed that of the white population.[24] By contrast, the Irish can be said to be among the most politically successful of United States ethnic groups; yet by *every* measure of socioeconomic status they do not compare favorably to the Japanese or Jews or Chinese.

The history of ethnic minorities in the United States, and elsewhere, seriously calls into question those premises that argue that disadvantaged minorities in the United States *must* acquire political power and undertake programs to "end racism" in order for socioeconomic growth to occur. The importance of recognizing that political power and/or social benevolence may not be a necessary condition for the socioeconomic progress of an ethnic group is not only a significant intellectual exercise but is of practical importance as well because all activities require resource expenditure. If resources are spent for political organization, for example, that means that those same resources cannot be spent, perhaps more usefully, elsewhere.

Intergroup Relations

When one discusses racial relationships, at some point the conversation usually turns to concepts involving patterns among different racial groups, i.e., integration and segregation. This issue has become the focal point of legislative bodies, courts and civil rights activists (school integration, residential integration and employment integration). In areas of civil rights activity where integration and an equal opportunity policy are translated into racial goals, targets and quotas, the notion that blacks, Mexican-Americans, Indians and Puerto Ricans may have preferences that are at variance with statistical laws of nature or have preferences that produce racial patterns inconsistent with preconceived notions of social scientists and judges escapes many people. Many people assume that the existence of homogeneous association is evidence of racial injustice or racial exclusion. This point of view implicitly assumes that, in the absence of racial injustice or exclusion, *voluntary* individual action would not produce today's pattern of homogeneous groupings by race.

Whether homogeneous grouping by race reflects racial injustice or social conditions that we should change raises important questions for social scientists and policy-makers alike. How much does racial grouping reflect voluntary individual or group behavior? How much does racial grouping reflect institutional restraints on individual or group choice?

Homogeneous grouping or sorting, in general, can take place along many lines. Groups develop where the shared common characteristic appears to be language, age, sex, color, religion, income, comparative advantage, education, etc. Some grouping obviously results from various laws; for example, racially restrictive housing covenants may produce certain well-defined racial land-use patterns where one race of people may reside solely in one area. However, some voluntary grouping results from individual characteristics such as age. For example, one does not expect to find senior citizens enrolled in kindergarten classes. Other kinds of homogeneous grouping are of a more complex nature but very simple in their primary component parts. The poor become separated from the rich, the low-skilled from the high-skilled, the less educated from the more educated, and so forth.

For various reasons, race is correlated with income and education. Therefore, *even if* there were no collectively organized racial separation of blacks, Puerto Ricans, and Mexican-Americans in housing or employment, these minorities might not be randomly distributed in terms of residences and employment. Nor would they be distributed by some preconceived notion of what is required for justice. The reason is that education is correlated to skill level; skill level is correlated with income; and income is correlated with residence.

Nothing here is being said to minimize the effects of economic, as opposed to racial, grouping. Instead, the recognition is being made that *unorganized* individual behavior often gets transformed into "apparently" organized results. But there are a large number of collective results that operate independently of individual motivation or intent which are widely known. For example, the phenomena of pile-ups of a large number of automobiles, or even two-car accidents, are commonplace events that operate independently of individual desires. Dating and marriage are essentially private activities; yet the income and genetic implications of the persons involved produce certain collective results. No couple marries with the intent of maintaining or increasing the skewness of the income distribution. But the fact that the rich tend to marry the rich, the intelligent marry the intelligent and the educated marry the educated seems to reinforce income differentials between groups of people. Neither do couples purposely intend to increase the genetic randomization in the population when girls seek men who are taller than themselves.

In the realm of economic activity, there are collective results produced by individual action that cannot be traced to individual intent. The most familiar are depressions and inflations. The actions of millions of consumers that produce a depression or an inflation cannot be traced to individual desires to earn lower income or to pay higher prices.

The fact that collective behavior may not result from

individual intentions (or racial motivation) should compel the student of race relations to examine more carefully the meaning of racial patterns. And even where human intent is found to be the cause of a collective phenomenon that has a racial character, we should ask whether the phenomenon is a result of racial tastes or some other set of motives. Or more generally, we should ask: If man does not exhibit random association, what attributes serve as a basis for various types of grouping? What are the kinds of incentives that produce homogeneous grouping? When the questions are asked in this way, it is by no means clear that race is the most important criterion upon which associative relationships are formed.

Residential Grouping

Residential racial grouping is a common form of racial association in the United States. This is a fact even though there has been *general compliance* with laws that prohibit people from refusing to sell real estate on racial grounds despite the fact that relatively few resources have been allocated to the enforcement of these laws.[25] The fact that racially homogeneous neighborhoods persist in the face of general compliance with nondiscriminatory housing laws suggests that these patterns are just the visual component of a far more complex grouping pattern.

Buying a house is not just the purchasing of a physical property; it is the "purchasing" of neighbors, shopping centers, schools, playgrounds and a host of other publicly financed services such as fire and crime protection and refuse collection. Economists often refer to a house as a composite good, which differs from, say, a car. When one purchases a house, he simultaneously makes a decision about his consumption and expenditure level for a number of publicly financed goods. The cost of public goods such as schools, playgrounds and refuse collection are reflected in the purchase price of the house and the local property taxes. People's preferences for public goods as well as private goods differ and may differ systematically with income. However, the implications of taste differences for public goods are not the same as those for private goods. For private goods, it pays the individual to enter the market to exchange with people whose tastes are *different* from his own.[26] For example, a boy possessing Yankee cards, but desiring Dodger cards, will achieve a higher level of satisfaction if he finds another boy possessing Dodger cards but desiring Yankee cards. Or when we shop, we seek people (merchants) who wish to get rid of food in exchange for money while we wish to get rid of money in exchange for food.

However, in the case of publicly financed goods, it pays him to associate with persons whose tastes and means are *similar* to his own. This is because of the characteristics of some publicly financed goods. Most publicly produced goods, because of their nature, must be provided in approximately equal levels within the particular locality. A group of individuals with similar tastes for public goods (and similar means for paying) are likely to experience lower decision-making costs and fewer political hassles as a result of their basic agreement on objectives. For example, a heterogeneous community, say, that of retired senior citizens *and* young married couples, may encounter conflict and hence high decision-making costs on an issue such as the number of schools to finance with a property tax levied on all residents. Obviously, the people with school-age children would prefer a larger expenditure on school support than those without school-age children.

Therefore, it is efficient for people with similar tastes and the means to pay for public goods to reside together. If communities exhibit a high degree of homogeneity, it is less likely that local budget and expenditure decisions will be highly offensive to any one individual's set of tastes.[27] This theoretical proposition regarding homogeneous association is reinforced by studies of sociologists and demographers. Reynolds Farley reports, "Once a suburb is established, the population that moves into that suburb tends to resemble the population already living there."[28]

In effect, the choice of residence becomes a method for the registering of tastes for public goods such as schools.

The presence of many local political jurisdictions that provide different kinds, quantities and qualities of public goods enables households to achieve the desired mix of public goods, given their means, in a way that minimizes conflict. Therefore, we expect to find income and residence, independent of any other factor (including race), highly correlated. Also, to the extent that residents want to minimize individual expenditures for a given quantity of local services, they have an incentive to exclude from use those who add to costs but do not bear the full share of the tax burden. Localities use a number of devices for ensuring that everyone pays his share of the cost; zoning ordinances are a prime tool for this purpose.

Exclusion techniques utilized by local jurisdictions ultimately take the shape of those based on income. The fact that race is correlated with income should make it not surprising nor difficult to reconcile the fact of a relatively small number of blacks in the suburbs *and* the absence of organized behavior to keep blacks out. The absence of blacks is consistent with either community indifference, malevolence or benevolence toward blacks as a group.

Race or Class?

Negroes are entering the economic mainstream of American life in unprecedented numbers. In some respects this provides something of a laboratory by which we can evaluate arguments that use racial tastes (or racial injustice) as the explanation for certain racial patterns in society. We can for the first time ask: Do Negroes and whites differ significantly in their associative patterns when they are similar in socioeconomic characteristics other than race?

First, consider residential patterns and neighborhood preferences of blacks and whites. Middle-class suburbanites have categorically rejected federally subsidized "scatter-site" low-income housing in the suburbs. The resistance to low-income housing sites in the suburbs is attributed in many minds to anti-Negro sentiments of the white middle class.[29] The purely racial aspect of the motivation for the exclusion of low-income housing loses some of its credibility when we consider the evidence.

A Gallup poll in 1972 asked middle-class whites what they thought of letting lower-class whites and blacks move into their neighborhoods. The results were significant: 44 percent resented lower-class blacks moving in while 37 percent resented lower-class whites moving in. But blacks of the same middle-class status were resented by only 24 percent. White middle-class people clearly preferred a black neighbor of their own status to a white who was of a lower class.[30] These survey results take on greater significance if they are compared with those in the early 1940s. To the question: "If a Negro with just as much income and education as you have moved into your block, would it make a difference to you?" the National Opinion Research Center found that 65 percent of the respondents would object.[31]

These surveys definitely indicate important changes in white attitudes toward blacks.[32] This trend interestingly enough continued through the 1960s in spite of the much publicized riot-oriented "white backlash," which did not materialize in the survey data.

Only a few suburbs contain a large number of blacks. However, as a result of increasing economic progress and a complete collapse of restrictive covenants, blacks are finding their ways into the suburbs in increasing numbers. There is evidence that Negro suburban families entertain the same fears of the incursion of low-income families for the same stated reasons as white suburbanites. In the town of North Hempstead on Long Island, black family organized opposition led to the killing of a federally-subsidized low-income housing project. The reasons that the *black* families gave for their opposition was that they felt that neighborhood deterioration would take place and the quality of life would change.[33]

It appears that middle-class black families will resist federally-subsidized low-income housing just as middle-class white families will, in spite of the fact that the occupants of the low-income housing may be fellow blacks. In fact, a key court decision limiting low-income housing subsi-

dies in a predominantly black middle-class area was brought
by *blacks* (*Shannon* v. *Hud*, 436 F. 2d. 809, 3d. Cir. 1970).
Other cases where *blacks* brought suit against federally-subsidized housing in black middle-class neighborhoods are:
Banks v. *Perk*, 341 F. Supp. 1175 (N.D. Ohio, 1972); *Hicks*
v. *Weaver*, 302 F. Suppl. 619 (E.D. La. 1969).

Open-housing advocates and their new allies, builders
and developers, are making through the courts an assault
on zoning and other restrictive land use practices. Not sur-
prisingly, they found *middle-class blacks* allied with middle-
class whites as their opponents to subsidized low-income
housing in the suburbs.[34]

These findings suggest that what may appear to be a
racial phenomenon (such as suburban rejection of low-income housing) may instead be an economic or social class
phenomenon. But even more importantly, from a policy per-
spective, the findings point up the danger of equating white
with high incomes and black with low incomes. Today, in
light of unprecedented economic gains being made by
blacks, such an equation increasingly does not apply.

Another phenomenon that has been suggested to be racially motivated is "white flight" to the suburbs. What has
recently become a concern of many cities with large black
populations such as Chicago, Boston, New York, Washington, D.C., Newark, and elsewhere is *black* flight to the
suburbs.[35] The reasons given by blacks for their unprecedented movement to the suburbs are quite similar to those
given by whites who have moved to the suburbs, such as
better schooling, fear of crime, and the declining quality
of city life.[36] Again, this behavior on the part of blacks weak-
ens the aspect of suburban flight purportedly motivated by
racial tastes.[37]

That residential patterns *per se* cannot be *fully* accounted for by racial discrimination is revealed by examining residential patterns of Negroes within areas of their
highest concentration. One question that can be asked is:
Does residential segregation, according to social class, exist
within a color group? More particularly, are social classes
segregated within Negro ghettos? Or are the forces of racial

Table 1

Percentage with Family Income of $7,000 or More in 1959, by Distance from Central Business District, Nonwhite Families, 24 Selected Cities, 1960[a,b]

	NORTH								SOUTHWEST		WEST		
MILES	New York	Chicago	Detroit	Philadelphia	Cleveland	Indianapolis	Newark	Buffalo	Dallas	Houston	San Francisco	Oakland	Los Angeles
0–1	9.3 }	12.2 }	3.3	8.2	11.8	11.4	13.5	7.9	5.5 }	4.2	29.6	14.3	14.8 }
1–2	9.3	12.2	6.7	12.4	10.8	15.2	17.5	12.5	5.5	8.2	23.6	15.2	14.8
2–3	12.8	11.8	10.7	15.4	19.1	16.1	33.8	22.1	7.9	19.6	32.8	26.3	19.3
3–4	13.6	16.2	15.7	26.1	29.3	25.9	37.4	32.3	5.5	7.2	26.7	27.3	21.8
4–5	18.8	20.4	24.2	26.2	36.0	46.0			5.0	8.6	40.8	31.0	29.8
5–6	18.8	27.9	23.7	29.8	46.1					10.8	50.5	37.8	34.3
6–7	22.5	26.8	27.3	37.5								27.2	35.6
7–8	15.0	27.7	30.8										24.1
8–9	11.3	41.2											16.3
9–10	—	50.4											29.5
10–11	25.6	45.6											
11–12	40.0	54.6											
12–13	46.9												

SOUTH

MILES	BORDER Washington, D.C.	St. Louis	Kansas City	Baltimore	Cincinnati	Louisville	SOUTH Atlanta	Richmond	New Orleans	Birmingham	Memphis
0-1	12.6	1.8	4.2	7.0	4.7	4.0	5.1	4.0	5.5	2.3	1.9
1-2	19.1	4.1	7.9	11.2	9.6	8.3	8.0	10.9	6.5	8.2	4.2
2-3	24.4	9.4	17.4	21.2	18.1	12.7	10.6	10.4	10.3	10.5	5.4
3-4	35.1	15.7	17.3	27.5	29.1	16.1	14.9	10.4	8.7	8.0	8.0
4-5	41.0	21.4	28.7							7.0	6.7
5-6	28.0									8.2	4.0

a Source: Schnore, *Demography*, p. 130.
b Underscoring represents highest percent in column.

discrimination strong enough to force Negroes of different socioeconomic classes to live side by side?

Leo F. Schnore conducted a study of 24 major metropolitan areas with large contiguous areas of Negro residents.[38] He combined census tracts into zones that had a radial distance of one-mile intervals from the center of the city. The research question was to find the percentage of Negro families with incomes over $7,000 per year as a function of miles from the center of the city. The study found that "as distance increases from the center of the city, the socioeconomic status of nonwhite neighborhoods rises. Nonwhite family income is higher, nonwhite educational levels mount, and the relative number of nonwhite males in "white-collar" employment increases."[39] In Table 1, these findings are presented for Schnore's 24 cities. It shows a consistent pattern for most of the cities studied; in some cities (e.g., Los Angeles) there are some problems of interpretation because of peculiarities in the legal city boundaries. These findings also point to the inescapable conclusion that collective behavior that produces homogeneous association is not necessarily indicative of *racial* discrimination.

The point of this discussion is *not* to minimize the effects of residential grouping attributable to economic or class differences; nor is the assertion made that racial discrimination is nonexistent in housing. But we know that housing patterns depend upon at least three *different* factors: the first is racial discrimination; the second is economic restraints that limit the quantity and quality of housing that can be purchased; and the third is individual taste. All three influence the choice of neighborhood. The recognition that residential housing patterns are a result of the interaction of these, and perhaps other factors, may help us to overcome the error of assuming that the absence of a proportional residential distribution of blacks is necessarily indicative of racial discrimination. Determining which factors play what roles and which factors are more important than others is no small statistical task. To design a test that will give us such knowledge may even be impossible. However, the recognition that racial residential patterns are influenced by several variables should compel us to realize that government programs to integrate housing forcefully may undo far more than what racial discrimination, alone, has created.

The courts, possibly recognizing this phenomenon, have not usually ordered metropolitan remedies for strictly city problems. Perhaps the clearest statement of this position was *Milliken* v. *Bradley,*[40] which upheld the long-standing federal equity principle that the nature of the violation determines the scope of the remedy. The Court said that without an interdistrict violation, there is no basis for an interdistrict remedy—in short, that the school districts of Detroit and its environs could not be ordered consolidated for the purposes of achieving racial balance.

However, the courts have been equivocal in the application of the federal equity principle. In *Metropolitan Housing Development* v. *Village Heights,*[41] the court said, "Whenever a *de facto* condition of segregation exists, a municipality—regardless of its involvement in the condition of segregation—is constitutionally obligated to ease the problem by affirmative action." The court went on to say, "Merely because Arlington Heights did not create the problem does not necessarily mean that it can ignore it."[42] In the more recent *H.U.D.* v. *Gatreaux* Supreme Court decision, upholding a lower court decision, the Court said, "Nothing in the Milliken decision suggests a per se rule that Federal courts lack authority to order parties found to have violated the constitution to undertake remedial efforts beyond the municipal boundaries of the city where the violation occurred."[43]

Summary

In this chapter, we have discussed a number of popularly believed statements about racial discrimination which have taken on the status of axiomatic truths. We have presented brief accounts of ethnic minorities, both in the United States and elsewhere, which suggest (1) that social benevolence is not a *necessary* condition for minority socioeconomic progress and (2) that political power is not a necessary condition for economic advance.

We have also argued that homogeneous association by race does not require, as its antecedent, malevolent majority preferences for minorities. In the housing market model that we discussed, it was shown how *unorganized* individual behavior gets transformed into "apparently" organized results, i.e., ethnically homogeneous communities. However, an example of some of the nonracial considerations surrounding housing choice and community behavior, we presented evidence that Negroes who were suburban residents exhibited behavior quite similar to that of whites. This observation tends to weaken the purely racial hypothesis of homogeneous grouping.

The importance of all of this, and a guiding point to all of our discussion, is that effective policy to remedy the legacy of racial oppression requires correct identification of cause and effect. In the next chapter we will discuss what we believe accounts for much of the confusion surrounding racial issues, which is the imprecise and value-ladened terminology that is used to analyze racial relationships. The object of the discussion is not to *justify* different behavioral forms but to set up an effective way, free of emotions, by which we may better analyze racial relationships.

CHAPTER 2

Racial Terminology and Confusion

Error is never so difficult to be destroyed as when it has roots in language.

—Jeremy Bentham

WORDS CAN, and usually do, have more than one meaning and therefore can be used ambiguously. Without a doubt, part of the confusion in understanding racial problems stems from the imprecise and ambiguous language used by scholars and laymen alike in discussing race. In analytical usage not only is it necessary to separate the connotative from the literal content of words, but precise and operationally useful distinctions and definitions must be made.

A good example of shifting definitions is found in the usage of the phrase "racial segregation." If the average American were asked: Are public water fountains, libraries and theaters of the U.S. desegregated? a broad, if not unanimous, consensus would be reached that they were indeed desegregated. Then ask the average American whether the country's public schools are desegregated. For this question, a consensus on any one answer would be virtually impossible. In fact, there are many legal actions charging that schools are segregated and there are just as many claiming that the schools are not segregated.

A little thought on the matter shows that the term racial segregation means one thing when applied to water fountains, libraries and theaters. Racial segregation means quite another thing when applied to schools, jobs and housing. In the case of water fountains, desegregation means that if a black is at a water fountain and desires to drink, he is free to do so. In the case of public schools, desegregation "means" that the number of blacks in attendance is some preconceived percentage, say 12 percent, of those in attendance. If the preconceived numerical figure is not realized, then remedial measures are proposed or legislated. No one ever bothers to apply a similar numerical test to establish whether water fountains, libraries and theaters are desegregated. And surely no one proposes busing blacks to all white water fountains, libraries and theaters for the purpose of promoting "social justice."

There are other terms and concepts used in the racial literature and debate which are just as misleading and confusing. The aim of this chapter is to point out the ambiguities and suggest operational definitions to see whether more light can be shed on public policy analysis.

Racial Preferences

People may have likes or dislikes or be indifferent toward many objects of desire. In everyday language as well as in economic analysis, an individual is said to prefer object A to object B if he places a higher value on A than on B. In economic theory, we postulate that each individual has a consistent set of preferences—that is, tastes—and chooses the combination he most prefers from the available alternatives. When we are speaking as economists, there are no objective criteria by which we can judge whether one set of preferences is "better" than another. We cannot prove, for example, that it is better or more righteous for a person to prefer the wines of Bordeaux to those of Burgundy or to prefer blue cars to red cars. The most we can ever say objectively is that, given his preference pattern and income and price constraints, the chooser is—or is not—doing the best he can.

This holds true as well when we come to individual preferences for physical attributes such as height, weight, "richly" endowed body, hair color, and so forth: these are solely matters of individual taste. And given that there are individual preferences for or against physical attributes in general, we expect people to exhibit preferences for or against racial attributes as well. Indeed, so far as our analysis is concerned, there are no conceptual distinctions between racial and other preferences.

It may be rejoined that racial preferences are not comparable to other kinds of preferences in the consequences they have for society and for individuals. However, although the indulgence of racial preferences has specific effects that the indulgence of preferences for certain wines does not have, are the preferences basically different? If so, how do they differ? The preference for Bordeaux wines "harms" Burgundy producers by reducing the value of resources that are held for Burgundy production. If the consequences of preferences are generally thought to reduce the value of some resources and increase the value of others, then it can be said that preferences for physical attributes have effects similar to those of other preferences. The essential difference—by no means small—between preferences for racial features and those for wines is that the latter are not as specialized as the former. In other words, if Burgundy producers see that consumers prefer Bordeaux, they will try to shift their resources to Bordeaux production. On the other hand, for example, people who are black cannot become white.[1]

But the fact that racial characteristics are unchangeable does not put them in a class by themselves. Persons with average IQs are preferred to those with below-average IQs, and persons who are not physically disabled are preferred to those who are. In each of these cases the less-preferred characteristic is unchangeable and in each the less-preferred person suffers a competitive disadvantage. This disadvantage is to be expected. Disadvantage and advantage are inevitable consequences of differences in individual tastes, abilities, and traits, on the one hand, and freedom of choice in a democratic society, on the other.

Racial Prejudice

In the literature on race, prejudice is usually interpreted as meaning suspicion, intolerance or an irrational hatred of other races. Such an interpretation exposes the analysts to the pitfall of making ambiguous statements and advancing faulty logic. A more useful interpretation of "prejudice" can be found by looking to its Latin root meaning "to judge before." Therefore, a prejudiced act may be thus defined as a decision made on the basis of incomplete information. Making decisions without *complete* information is necessary in a world of scarcity and uncertainty. Another common experience in a complex world is erroneous interpretation of the evidence. Moreover, different individuals may arrive at different conclusions even if confronted with the *same* evidence. Furthermore, any given individual may sometimes be quite unresponsive to changes in the evidence.

Consider a simple, yet intuitively appealing, example of how decisions are made on the basis of incomplete information (and perhaps erroneous interpretation of evidence). Suppose a fully grown tiger suddenly appeared in the room. A reliable prediction is that most individuals would endeavor to leave the area with great dispatch. In most instances, the individual response to the tiger's presence is not based on detailed information about the behavioral characteristics of that *particular* tiger. Instead, the response is based on the individual's stock of information and perhaps misinformation about tigers as a class. The response is based on a stereotype; the individual makes a prejudiced decision. He makes no attempt to seek additional information but rather ascribes known or surmised group characteristics to the individual tiger. There abound examples of prejudiced behavior: not talking to strangers, running in response to rustling in the bushes, not buying dented cans of food, not recruiting employees from certain schools.

Decisions to prejudge are inextricably tied to individual judgments on what constitutes the right amount of information search. Information is not a free good; it is acquired by the expenditure of time, effort and usually money. As a result, individuals can be expected to economize on information costs. For any of us, there will be a point at which the cost of acquiring one more unit of information is equal to the expected total gain from that unit. This means that additional information will not be sought because the total cost would be greater than the added gain.

A vast number of decisions must be made during our lives. Some of them, such as deciding to greet a passerby in the morning, require relatively small amounts of information. Others, such as selecting a marriage partner, require relatively larger amounts. A person is not prejudiced or unprejudiced. Rather, a person always exhibits prejudiced behavior to the extent that he substitutes general information (prejudgment or stereotypes)—which is less costly—for more costly specific information. What distinguishes different people are their comparative degrees of prejudiced behavior when facing similar situations; some people will get more information than others prior to a decision.

In the literature on racial behavior, the word "prejudiced" is most often used pejoratively to refer to those whose optimum quantity of information is deemed by the observer to be too small. Behavior based on racial or sexual stereotypes is commonly viewed as making use of too little information and thus viewed as opprobrious—and in many cases, of course, it is illegal. However, the quantity of information effectively collected before decisions are made is up to the individual's calculation: for there is no social standard or optimum amount of search that is applicable to all individuals in all cases. For example, for the prospective house buyer there is no socially determined optimum number of houses to be canvassed before making a decision. Instead, the amount of information collected by free individuals before acting is determined by and reflects, among other things, the skill of the individual in converting resources into information. The value of those resources is measured against the expected value of a "correct" decision.

Since all of us will seek to economize on information expense, we will tend to substitute less costly forms of information for more costly forms. Physical attributes are easily observed and hence constitute a cheap form of information. If a particular physical attribute is highly correlated with some less easily observed attribute, then the physical attribute may be used as an estimator or proxy for the other. The cheaply observed fact that an individual is short, or an amputee, or a Negro, or a woman provides what some people deem "sufficient" information for predicting the presence of some other unobserved attribute under certain circumstances. Most of us, for example, if asked to identify individuals with advanced academic degrees *only* by observing race and sex, would assign a higher probability that white males would have such degrees than black males or women. Such behavior is what decision theory expects where *unobservable* variables must be estimated from *observable* variables.

Racial Discrimination

Discrimination may be defined as an act of choice based upon utility maximization. Racial discrimination is an act of choice whereby racial attributes provide the criteria for choice. In this view, racial discrimination does not differ in any fundamental sense from other kinds of discrimination. All selection necessarily and simultaneously requires nonselection; choice requires discrimination. When we preface the word "discrimination" with the word "racial," all we do is to state the attributes selected as the criteria for choice.

Our lives are largely spent discriminating for and against selected activities, objects and people. For example, many of us discriminate against those who have criminal records, who bathe infrequently, who use vulgar speech. Some employers discriminate against applicants who speak with a foreign accent, who have a low intelligence or cannot read or went to the "wrong" college. There is also evidence of discrimination in politics. Not many short men have been elected to the United States Presidency. Furthermore, personal discrimination is not consistent. Sometimes people discriminate against theater in favor of parties, against women in favor of men; and at other times the *same* people do the reverse.

When a choice is made on the basis of race, that choice *may* reflect the preferences of the chooser for a particular race, but it also *may not*. It is impossible for an observer to say for sure whether choices based on a particular physical feature reflect the indulgence of preference (tastes) *or* the attempt to minimize information costs (prejudice) *or* the recognition of real differences.

Prejudice in Action

Some may think my discussion of discrimination and prejudice renders the words meaningless, since it can be said that all human acts involve choice and all choices are based on incomplete information (as well as on tastes). But the discussion is useful because it permits us to avoid confusing one form of behavior with another. It enables us to see that certain kinds of choices—those made on the basis of racial, sexual and other physical attributes—may be intelligent optimizing or may be the result of tastes. An example will clarify these points.

Suppose we are on a university campus where the racial and sexual composition of the student body is the same as that of the U.S. population, and suppose we play a game of trying to identify students who can find the integral for the mathematical expression $\int x^2 dx$. Players are given *zero* information about the students' mathematical proficiency and may not communicate with students except to ask, "What is the integral?" In other words, players can distinguish between students only by observable attributes such as race, sex, mannerisms, dress and speech accent. The payoff from the game is $2,000 for each student *chosen by the player* who answers correctly and the player loses $200 for each student that he chooses who does not know the answer. Finally, it is assumed that the payoff is sufficient to induce participation and the player's sole objective is to maximize his winnings.

The player is in a situation where choices must be made

on the basis of incomplete information. He is faced with identifying those observable attributes that will be the best indicators of student proficiency in calculus (the unknown and unobservable attribute). If he thinks that mathematical proficiency is equally distributed by physical attributes, his choice process will be essentially random. But if he thinks that mathematical proficiency is not randomly distributed, he must adopt a different (nonrandom) decision rule. In his first cut at such a rule, he may decide not to choose females because he knows that women are not well represented in the quantitative sciences. (Note that such a rule might not be as valuable in the Soviet Union, where a greater portion of women enter the quantitative sciences.) In successive cuts at a decision rule, the player may discriminate against— not choose—Negroes, Puerto Ricans, and American Indians, perhaps reflecting his awareness that math skills are related to the quality of pre-college schooling and that these particular minorities have historically received grossly inferior elementary and secondary education. In the end the player may settle on a rule that confines his choices to males of Jewish or Oriental ancestry.

The fact that the choice may be made on the basis of race and sex is not the same as saying that there is a *genetic* or *causal* relationship between race or sex and mathematical proficiency. What is said is that these variables are *correlated* in the real world.[2]

Suppose we relax the implicit assumption of neutral racial preferences and assume that instead the player has a dislike for Jews and Orientals but still believes these groups to be disproportionately represented in the quantitative sciences. So long as we retain the assumption that the player seeks to maximize winnings, his decision rule, his prejudice, will not be distinguishable from that of a player with no particular racial preferences.

This illustrates an important point that is lost in most discussions of racial issues: choices made on the basis of race (or sex) do not always permit us to put the preferences of the chooser in unambiguous categories. Moreover, the example raises a question whether anyone should care if the player in the game chose to indulge his preference and not select Jews or Orientals? In our scenario (assuming that Jews and Orientals are disproportionately represented in the class of individuals knowing calculus), the player who because of tastes discriminated against Jews and Orientals would win less than other players. Even the most fervent advocate of civil rights would have little reason to seek a social policy that required anti-Jewish or anti-Oriental players to give Jews and Orientals an equal opportunity to be selected. The racist (or, for that matter, any individual who permitted his choices to be determined by economically irrelevant "preferences" of whatever kind) would bear the full cost of such an action. He would lose money.

Racial Preference, Optimizing Prejudice or Real Differences?

For some reason these points get lost in discussions of racial discrimination. We overlook the fact that not every discriminatory action reflects dislike of Negroes. For example: certain discrimination may come from the rational behavior of individuals minimizing information costs or confronting real differences in the market, whether that market is free or institutionally constrained. And we often overlook the fact that in a free market economically irrational preferences will impose costs on whoever indulges them. Institutional restraints may render that indulgence costless to the indulger. If they do, the answer is to lift the restraints and reimpose the costs. In other words, to free the market.

When we are formulating policy, we must be careful to distinguish among the three sources of "discrimination"— preference, prejudice and real differences. If we assume that racial tastes cause the problem we are addressing, when in fact the problem is caused by something else, our policy will be at least ineffectual and quite possibly harmful to its intended beneficiaries. Let us briefly look here at three areas where whites are generally charged with discrimination against blacks, and where the assumption is generally made that the discrimination is based on racial preferences.

These areas are hiring, home mortgages and the prices ghetto shoppers pay.

Hiring and Employment Discrimination

Many recruitment and hiring practices are said to reflect racial preference, but an alternative explanation can be drawn from our knowledge of hiring procedures. When a firm seeks labor, it must find out how productive those seeking jobs are likely to be and must train the persons it hires. Since this process costs money, the firm has incentive to search for recruits that appear to have a high probability of success. If the firm believes there is an important relationship between a recruit's high school performance (and the quality of his high school), on the one hand, and employee productivity, on the other, it can reduce some of its recruitment costs just by knowing the job candidate's record (and high school). If a firm knows that blacks at grade twelve (regardless of transcript grades) are frequently three to five years behind whites in scholastic achievement, it can assign a higher probability to a white recruit's having the desired productivity.

In the mind of the employer, skin color may be a first indicator of expected worker productivity. To observe a process that selects in part by skin color and to attribute the selection to taste (in this case, to employer "racism") would be misleading. It would be like concluding that auto insurance companies charge drivers under twenty-five years of age higher premiums because companies dislike them. Or that life insurance companies charge women lower premiums because the companies like women better than men. In both cases, a physical attribute may act as a general proxy for some other attribute (in the case of drivers, the higher probability of an accident) that is individually more costly to ascertain.

Suppose an employer who has racially neutral preferences incorrectly perceives that, on the average, a Negro worker is less productive than a white worker. What kinds of laws would cause him to seek more information and perhaps revise his perception? And what kinds of laws would discourage him from doing so? Clearly, laws that require him to pay all workers identical wages or laws that make it very costly to fire an employee. The reason is that laws or union rules that mandate a certain specified pay for a particular job reduce the incentive for experimentation. The employer quite rationally hires that employee whom he perceives as more productive. The basis for the perception can be sex, race, accent, demeanor, school and other factors. The existence of laws or union rules that make it difficult to fire a worker reinforces the reluctance of employers to experiment in hiring. The reason is that the employer feels that if his experimentation turns out to be a mistake, he has to incur additional costs to reverse the error.

This kind of behavior by employers is just a special case of a general principle that all people employ in their conduct. A brief example will demonstrate it. Suppose a new, unheard of supermarket located in an area in the presence of established supermarkets. How would it entice customers (employers of food) to try it out? The standard way is to offer "sales," i.e., sell some of its merchandise at a lower price than charged elsewhere. Customers have additional inducement to experiment with the new supermarket because if they are dissatisfied they need not come back; i.e., they "fire" the supermarket. Now suppose there is some law or rule (1) requiring that all supermarkets charge the same price and (2) stipulating that once a customer chose a supermarket he had to stick with it; he could not "fire" it. The response of customers to the new supermarket would be obvious: Why try it?

Home Mortgage Discrimination

Some of the principles discussed in this chapter apply to redlining, a practice whereby banks and other lending institutions refuse to grant mortgages for homes in certain neighborhoods. Because the practice most often applies to minority inner-city poor neighborhoods, the national debate about it has focused on its racial aspects, with banks being labeled as racist.

Forgotten in much of the debate is the existence of regulations that place ceilings on the interest rates banks can charge for home mortgages. Given these ceilings, banks have an incentive to ration credit, namely to lend money to those whose perceived credit worthiness is appropriate to the permitted legal interest rate. It turns out that, for a number of reasons, the probability of default per dollar lent is greater in some neighborhoods than in others. Moreover, several laws designed to protect borrowers make the collection and eviction of debtors who are in default more costly to bankers. These circumstances reduce the probability of earning normal profits in some neighborhoods.

Thus, redlining need not be a result of bankers' racism. In many cases (perhaps almost all) it occurs not because bankers are unwilling to make home loans to inner-city blacks but because the inner city is not perceived as a profitable market at the state-imposed interest rate ceiling. The real villain in the redlining issue is the legislature that imposes, say, a 10 percent interest rate ceiling. Such a ceiling in effect says that if an applicant is not a good enough risk for a mortgage at 10 percent, he will not get a mortgage at all—although without a ceiling he may get a mortgage at a 15 percent rate. Interestingly, black-owned banks that do not find the ghetto an attractive place to make loans are not called racist, and we should note that more black-owned banks invest more of their loan portfolio *outside* the community in which they are located than do white-owned banks.[3]

Public policy directed at supposed banker racism will miss its mark and may, like affirmative action in lending, exacerbate the credit problems of blacks. Banks will simply move away. An effective policy would examine cost conditions in inner-city ghettos and remove or change state usury laws. Once again, what is prejudice or perhaps a recognition of real differences is misdiagnosed as "preference"—with predictably poor policy results.

Discrimination Against Poor Shoppers

During the mid-1960s it was widely alleged that white merchants in ghetto areas exploited their customers by charging higher prices and selling lower-quality merchandise there than they did elsewhere. The merchants, it was said, were trying to earn supranormal profits as a way of acting out their racial hostility toward Negroes.[4] But it turns out that racial hostility by merchants could not adequately explain ghetto prices.

Prices were indeed higher in ghetto areas, and several studies showed that retail food chains followed different pricing policies in ghetto and nonghetto areas. With these findings in hand, the Federal Trade Commission, along with consumer advocate groups and public interest lawyers, attempted, through public pressure, to require that ghetto merchants offer their customers the same terms of exchange they were offered in nonghetto areas.

But to view the merchants' behavior as exploitative or racist ignores the fact that ghettos tend to present a high-cost business environment. Losses from business-related crime are higher there than elsewhere as a percentage of total sales; business, fire and theft insurance premiums are also higher; and extension of credit is riskier. In addition, because of the low income of ghetto residents and its effect on sales mix and volume, merchandising techniques used to lower sales costs in nonghetto areas are not readily adaptable to ghetto areas. Much of the behavior that critics have condemned is merely an economic response to an environment that raises the cost of doing business. If products and services are to be provided in the ghetto, prices must reflect their higher costs.

Evidence substantiates this explanation of merchant behavior. The Federal Trade Commission has shown that while gross margins were higher in ghetto areas, the difference was more than accounted for by higher operating costs, and the return on equity was considerably lower in the ghetto than elsewhere.[5] The assertion that supranormal profits were earned becomes even less credible when we recognize that retailing is characterized by relative ease of entry, so that if supranormal profits existed, merchants would open new businesses until profits in ghetto and nonghetto areas were equalized. The opposite of this has occurred in urban areas: businesses have left without being replaced. Furthermore, none of those who attributed the prices charged by white merchants to racism noted that the prices charged by Negro merchants were about the same.

The crusade that blamed the problem of the ghetto consumer on the greed and racism of whites may well have reduced the welfare of the ghetto consumer. The adverse publicity and boycotts (and other actions) against merchants in ghetto communities gave these merchants increased reason to move out. The result is fewer neighborhood stores, with shoppers being forced to travel longer distances or pay even higher local prices than in the past.

Conclusion

The chapter has sought to give operational meaning to the terminology used in the analysis of race. There was also the attempt to extricate from race some of the emotive language. Dispassionate analysis and a clear meaning of language are two minimal requirements for effective policy.

In the next chapters, there will be more detailed discussion of what is the basic problem of blacks in America. This problem is: severe government-imposed restraints on voluntary exchange. Or put another way: the diminution of free markets in the United States.

CHAPTER 3

Minimum Wage, Maximum Folly

Of sentences that stir my bile,
  Of phrases I detest,
There's one beyond all others vile:
  "He did it for the best."

—James Kenneth Stephen
  The Malefactor's Plea

MOST LABOR MARKET ACTIVITY is regulated by some level of government. Well-meaning people put political pressures on government to enact laws they think will help disadvantaged people. One of the ways government regulates, "in the interest" of the disadvantaged, is through the setting of maximum and minimum prices at which transactions can legally occur. The imposition of maximum prices, as in the case of rent controls, and minimum prices, as in the case of wages, yields predictable economic results. Often the results are at considerable variance with the intentions of well-meaning people. In this chapter the results of the minimum wage will be analyzed.

The Fair Labor Standards Act was adopted by Congress in 1938. The act has been amended many times to increase the number of employees under its coverage and to increase the legal minimum wage. The most recent amendment, in 1977, provided for a minimum hourly wage in 1981 of $3.35. The federal minimum wage is complemented by state minimum wage laws that may exceed the federal minima. Federal and state minimum wage laws are acts of governmental intervention in the labor market which are intended to produce a pattern of events other than that produced in a free market. The legislated minima raise the wage to a level higher than that which would have occurred with free market forces.

Legislative bodies have the power to legislate a wage increase, but unfortunately, they have not found a way to legislate worker productivity increases. Further, while Congress can legislate the price of a labor transaction, it cannot require that the transaction actually be made. That is, they can dictate what minimum wage must be paid a person *if* you hire him, but they cannot dictate that you hire him in the first place. To the extent that the minimum wage law raises the pay level to that which may exceed the productivity of some workers, employers will predictably make adjustments in their use of labor.[1] Such an adjustment will produce gains for some workers at the expense of other workers. Those workers who retain their jobs and receive a higher wage clearly gain. The adverse effects are borne by those workers who are most disadvantaged in terms of marketable skills—those who lose their jobs and their income or who are not hired in the first place.

The effect of the minimum wage law is more clearly seen if we put ourselves in the place of an employer and ask: If a wage of $3.35 per hour must be paid no matter who is hired, what kind of worker does it pay to hire?[2] Clearly the answer, in terms of economic efficiency, is to hire workers whose productivity is the closest to $3.35 per hour. If such workers are available, it does not pay the firm to hire workers whose output is, say, $2 per hour. Even if the employer were willing to train such a worker, the fact that the worker must be paid a wage higher than the market value of his output plus the training cost makes on-the-job training an unattractive proposition.

The impact of legislated minima can be brought into sharper focus if we ask the distributional question: Who bears the burden of the minimum wage? As suggested earlier, the workers who bear the heaviest burden are those that are the most marginal. These are workers whom employers perceive as being less productive or more costly to employ than other workers. In the U.S. there are at least two segments of the labor force that share the marginal worker characteristics to a greater extent than do other segments of the labor force. The first group consists of youths in general. They are low-skilled or marginal because of their age, immaturity and lack of work experience. The second group, which contains members of the first group, are racial minorities such as Negroes and Hispanics, who, as a result of racial discrimination and a number of other socioeconomic factors, are disproportionately represented among low-skilled workers. These workers are not only made unemployable by the minimum wage, but their opportunities to upgrade their skills through on-the-job training are also severely limited.[3]

It is no accident that it is precisely these labor market participants who are also disproportionately represented among the unemployment statistics. Youth unemployment, even during relatively prosperous times, ranges from two to three times that of the general labor force. Black youth unemployment ranges from three to five times that of the general labor force. Black youth unemployment, nationally for more than a decade, had ranged from two to three times the unemployment rate for white youths. In some metropolitan areas it is reported that black youth unemployment exceeds 60 percent! The economic effects of minimum wage legislation have been analyzed in numerous statistical studies that could be read by the interested.[4] While there is some debate over the magnitude of the effects, the weight of academic research by economists points to the conclusion that unemployment for some population groups is directly related to legal minimum wages and that the unemployment effects of the minimum wage law are felt disproportionately by nonwhites. Professor Jacob Mincer, in an important statistical study of minimum wage laws, reports:[5]

> The net minimum wage effects on labor force participation appear to be negative for most of the groups. The largest negative effects are observed for nonwhite teenagers, followed by nonwhite males (20–24), white teenagers, and nonwhite males (25–64).

The net employment effects are negative within the exception of nonwhite females (20 plus), for whom the positive coefficient is statistically insignificant. The largest disemployment effects are observed for nonwhite teenagers, followed by nonwhite males (20–24), white teenagers, and white males (20–24).

Although most people are familiar with the recent statistics on black youth unemployment, not many are aware of the black/white youth employment statistics for earlier periods, which are included in Tables 2 and 3. In 1948 black youth unemployment was roughly the same as white youth unemployment. For that year, blacks aged sixteen to seventeen had an unemployment rate which was less than whites for the same age—9.4 percent unemployed compared with 10.2 percent whites unemployed. In the same period (until the mid-60s), black youths generally were either just as active in the labor force or more so than white youths. Since the sixties, both the labor force participation rate and the employment rate of black youths have fallen to what it is today. For black youths sixteen to seventeen years old, the labor force participation rate is now only 60 percent of that of white youths while earlier their labor force participation rate was higher than that of white youths.

Faced with these facts, one naturally asks why have labor market opportunities deteriorated so precipitously for black youth? Can racial discrimination explain this kind of reversal? Probably not. It would be a very difficult task for anyone to support the argument that employers have now become more racially discriminatory than they were in the past. Can we say that the lower unemployment for blacks in the past was because blacks had educational attainment levels equal to or higher than whites? No we cannot. The answer lies elsewhere. One of the answers is that reduced employment opportunities is one effect of minimum wage legislation.

But some supporters of the minimum wage law attempt to rebut this line of reasoning through another argument. For example, economist Professor Bernard Anderson says, "The minimum wage argument does not explain why black

Table 2
Male Civilian Labor Force Participation Ratio by Race, Age

		B/W MALES 16–17	B/W MALES 18–19	B/W MALES 20–24	B/W MALES 16 AND OVER
	1954	.99	1.11	1.05	1.00
	1955	1.00	1.01	1.05	1.00
1.00/hr	1956	.96	1.06	1.01	.99
	1957	.95	1.01	1.03	.99
	1958	.96	1.03	1.02	1.00
	1959	.92	1.02	1.04	1.00
	1960	.99	1.03	1.03	1.00
1.15/hr	1961	.96	1.06	1.02	.99
	1962	.93	1.04	1.03	.98
1.25/hr	1963	.87	1.02	1.04	.99
	1965	.88	1.01	1.05	.99
	1966	.87	.97	1.06	.98
1.40/hr	1967	.86	.95	1.04	.97
1.60/hr	1968	.79	.96	1.03	.97
	1969	.77	.95	1.02	.96
	1970	.71	.92	1.00	.96
	1971	.65	.87	.98	.94
	1972	.68	.85	.97	.93
	1973	.63	.85	.95	.93
2.00/hr	1974	.65	.85	.95	.92
2.10/hr	1975	.57	.79	.92	.91
2.30/hr	1976	.57	.77	.91	.90
	1977	.57	.77	.90	.90
2.65/hr	1978	.60	.79	.89	.92
2.90/hr	1979	.57	.78	.91	.91
3.10/hr	1980	.60	.76	.91	.90

Source: Computed from U.S. Department of Labor, Bureau of Labor Statistics, *Handbook of Labor Statistics 1975*—Reference ed. (Washington D.C.: Government Printing Office, 1975), pp. 36–37; U.S. Department of Labor, Bureau of Labor Statistics, *Employment and Unemployment in 1976;* Special Labor Force Report 199 (Washington, D.C.: Government Printing Office, 1977). 1978, '79, '80 figures obtained directly from Employment Analysis Division of U.S. Department of Labor.

Table 3

Comparison of Youth and General Unemployment by Race (Males)

YEAR	GENERAL	WHITE 16–17	BLACK 16–17	B/W RATIO	WHITE 18–19	BLACK 18–19	B/W RATIO	WHITE 20–24	BLACK 20–24	B/W RATIO
1948	3.8	10.2	9.4	.92	9.4	10.5	1.11	6.4	11.7	1.83
1949	5.9	13.4	15.8	1.18	14.2	17.1	1.20	9.8	15.8	1.61
*1950	5.3	13.4	12.1	.90	11.7	17.7	1.51	7.7	12.6	1.64
1951	3.3	9.5	8.7	.92	6.7	9.6	1.43	3.6	6.7	1.86
1952	3.0	10.9	8.0	.73	7.0	10.0	1.43	4.3	7.9	1.84
1953	2.9	8.9	8.3	.93	7.1	8.1	1.14	4.5	8.1	1.80
1954	5.5	14.0	13.4	.96	13.0	14.7	1.13	9.8	16.9	1.72
1955	4.4	12.2	14.8	1.21	10.4	12.9	1.24	7.0	12.4	1.77
*1956	4.1	11.2	15.7	1.40	9.7	14.9	1.54	6.1	12.0	1.97
1957	4.3	11.9	16.3	1.37	11.2	20.0	1.70	7.1	12.7	1.79
1958	6.8	14.9	27.1	1.81	16.5	26.7	1.62	11.7	19.5	1.66
1959	5.5	15.0	22.3	1.48	13.0	27.2	2.09	7.5	16.3	2.17
1960	5.5	14.6	22.7	1.55	13.5	25.1	1.86	8.3	13.1	1.58
*1961	6.7	16.5	31.0	1.89	15.1	23.9	1.58	10.0	15.3	1.53
1962	5.5	15.1	21.9	1.45	12.7	21.8	1.72	8.0	14.6	1.83
*1963	5.7	17.8	27.0	1.52	14.2	27.4	1.83	7.8	15.5	1.99
1964	5.2	16.1	25.9	1.61	13.4	23.1	1.72	7.4	12.6	1.70
1965	4.5	14.7	27.1	1.84	11.4	20.2	1.77	5.9	9.3	1.58
1966	3.8	12.5	22.5	1.80	8.9	20.5	2.30	4.1	7.9	1.93
*1967	3.8	12.7	28.9	2.26	9.0	20.1	2.23	4.2	8.0	1.90
*1968	3.6	12.3	26.6	2.16	8.2	19.0	2.31	4.6	8.3	1.80
1969	3.5	12.5	24.7	1.98	7.9	19.0	2.40	4.6	8.4	1.83
1970	4.9	15.7	27.8	1.77	12.0	23.1	1.93	7.8	12.6	1.62
1971	5.9	17.1	33.4	1.95	13.5	26.0	1.93	9.4	16.2	1.72
1972	5.6	16.4	35.1	2.14	12.4	26.2	2.11	8.5	14.7	1.73
1973	4.9	15.1	34.4	2.28	10.0	22.1	2.21	6.5	12.6	1.94
*1974	5.6	16.2	39.0	2.41	11.5	26.6	2.31	7.8	15.4	1.97
*1975	8.1	19.7	45.2	2.29	14.0	30.1	2.15	11.3	23.5	2.08
1976	7.0	19.7	40.6	2.06	15.5	35.5	2.29	10.9	22.4	2.05
1977	6.8	17.6	38.7	2.20	13.0	36.1	2.78	9.3	21.7	2.33
*1978	6.6	19.4	40.4	2.08	13.0	32.2	2.47	10.0	22.5	2.25
*1979	5.8	16.1	34.4	2.14	12.3	29.6	2.41	7.4	17.0	2.30
*1980	7.1	18.5	37.7	2.04	14.6	33.0	2.26	11.1	22.3	2.01

SOURCE: Adapted from Department of Labor, Bureau of Labor Statistics, *Handbook of Labor Statistics 1975*—Reference ed. (Washington, D.C.: Government Printing Office, 1975), pp. 153–55; U.S. Department of Labor, Bureau of Labor Statistics, *Employment and Unemployment in 1976*. Special Labor Force Report 199 (Washington, D.C.: Government Printing Office, 1977).

youths are so disproportionately affected; then why doesn't it reduce it as much for white youths as it does for black youths?"[6] This is not a refutation of economic theory about effects of the minimum wage. When wages are legislated that exceed the productivity of some workers, firms will make adjustment in their use of labor. One adjustment is to hire not only fewer youths, but to seek among those youths hired the more *highly qualified* youths. It turns out for a number of socioeconomic reasons that white youths, more often than black youths, have higher levels of educational attainment and training.[7] Therefore any law that discriminated against low-skilled people can be expected to confer a disproportionate burden on black youths compared with white youths.

Employer substitution of higher-skilled workers for lower-skilled workers, as discussed, is not the only effect of the minimum wage law. Minimum wages cause employers to make other kinds of substitution: machines for labor, changes in productive techniques and elimination of certain jobs altogether.

The substitution of automatic dishwashers for hand-washing and automatic tomato-picking machines for manual labor are examples of the substitution of machines for labor in response to higher wages. The switch from checkout ladies behind each counter in five-and-dime stores to cashiers and the switch from waiter-served restaurants to fast food restaurants are examples of changes-in-productive-technique response to higher wages. The absence of movie theater ushers and the wide usage of plastic and paperware utensils in restaurants are examples of the elimination-of-certain-jobs response to higher wages.

These are all possible and predictable responses to increases in the minimum wage law. Employers ask to economize on the usage of labor.

Minimum Wage and Racial Discrimination

"There is no job reservation left in the building industry, and in the circumstances I support the rate for the job as the second best way of protecting our white artisans."[8] "A year later, he stated that he would be prepared to allow black artisans into the industry provided that minimum wages were raised from Rand 1,40 to at least Rand 2,00 per hour and if the rate-for-the-job was strictly enforced."[9] These statements were made by the secretary of the avowedly racist Building Worker's Union, Gert Beetge. The question is why South Africa's racist unions support minimum wages and equal-pay-for-equal-work laws (rate-for-the-job) *for blacks!*

The racial effect of the minimum wage laws exists in the absence of racial preferences on behalf of employers. The minimum wage law gives firms effective economic incentive to seek to hire only the most productive employees, which means that firms are less willing to hire and/or train the least productive employee, which includes teenagers, particularly minority teenagers. But assuming away any productivity differences between black and white workers, minimum wage laws give firms incentive to racially discriminate in hiring. The reason is that the minimum wage law lowers the private cost of discriminating against the racially less preferred person.

The fact that a well-intentioned policy such as the minimum wage law can foster and promote racial discrimination is incomprehensible to some people. Therefore, it is useful to develop a nonracial example to illustrate the generality of the principle.

Take filet mignon and chuck steak. Assume that consumers, holding all else constant, prefer filet mignon to chuck steak, a not too unrealistic assumption. Then the question is: Why is it, in spite of consumer preferences, chuck steak sells at all? The actual fact of business is that chuck steak outsells (is more employed than) filet mignon! How does something less-liked compete with something more-liked?

It offers "compensating differences." In other words, as you wheel your shopping cart down the aisle, chuck steak, in effect, "says" to you, "I don't look as nice as filet mignon; I'm not as tender and tasty; but I'm not as expensive either." That is, chuck steak, by selling for $1.50 per pound, against filet mignon's $4 per pound, offers to "pay" you $2.50 for its "inferiority." Chuck steak pays you a compensating difference, which only means that it sells for a lower price.

Now suppose filet mignon, or a seller of filet mignon, wanted to collude against its less-preferred competitor, chuck steak, what would be its most effective strategy? Short of getting a law passed prohibiting sales of chuck steak, the best strategy would be that of a minimum steak law. What would be the effect of a minimum steak law of, say, $4 per pound of steak should the law be effectively enforced?

Again, put yourself in the position of the shopper wheeling the shopping cart down the aisle. Chuck steak "says" to you, "I don't look as nice as filet mignon, I'm not as tender and tasty, and I sell for the *same* price as filet mignon. Buy me." Such a message would fall on deaf ears. You would say to yourself, "Why should I buy chuck steak when it sells for the same price as filet mignon, which I like better anyway?" Such a sentiment reflects the basic law of demand. The lower the price of discriminating, the more of it will be done. The cost of discriminating against chuck steak, in the presence of the minimum steak law, is effectively zero. Whereas in the absence of the law, the cost of discriminating against chuck steak was $2.50 per pound, i.e., the difference in price.

We can now discuss how the minimum wage law encourages racial discrimination in the labor market through a similar mechanism. But first, a possible complaint about the analogy should be aired: people are not the same thing as cuts of meat. That is true just as a steel ball is not the same as a stone. But while steel balls and stones are different, *both* are influenced in the identical fashion by gravity. The independent influence of gravity on a steel ball's acceleration is 32 feet per second per second and its influence on a stone is 32 feet per second per second. Similarly, quantities demanded for cuts of meat are influenced by the law of demand and quantities demanded for labor services are influenced by that same law.

To understand how the minimum wage can raise the probability of employer preference indulgence and racial discrimination, we have to recognize that money income is not the only form of compensation businessmen earn.[10] The return from business consists of *non*money income as well. An employer prefers what *he* considers as desirable working conditions to less-desirable working conditions. In his estimation more-desirable working conditions may include finer furniture, plusher carpets, prettier secretaries and more likable employees. The amount of these "more-desirable working conditions" that he will choose depends on their costs.

Suppose that an employer has a preference for white employees over black employees. And for expository simplicity, assume the employees from which he chooses are identical in terms of their productivity. If there is a law, such as the minimum wage law, that requires that employers pay the same wage no matter who is hired, what are his incentives?[11] His incentives are that of preference indulgence. He must pay the black $3.35 per hour and he must pay the white $3.35 per hour. He must find some basis for choice. The minimum wage law says that his choice will not be based on economic criteria. Therefore, it must be based on noneconomic criteria. Race is a noneconomic criterion. If he wishes, the employer can discriminate against the black worker at zero cost. However, if there were no minimum wage and the black was willing to work for a lower wage, say $2 per hour, there would be positive costs to employer racial discrimination. In this example, it would be $1.35 per hour, the difference in wages per employee.

That's only one part of the story. The market would penalize the employer who chooses employees on market-irrelevant criteria.[12] There would be some employers who would hire blacks at the lower wage. Doing so and hence experiencing lower production costs, these firms would reap supernormal profits. Such a firm would be able to underprice the racially discriminating firms, thereby capturing a greater share of the market and attracting more investors. In addition, new firms may enter the scene, enticed by the profits. In their attempt to secure the cheaper black labor, they would offer higher wages. The effect would be that of wage equality between blacks and whites.[13] This line of reasoning is given additional weight when we consider black employment during relatively hostile times. During the "relatively unenlightened" times, black unemployment was lower and black labor force participation rates were higher than they are today. In 1910, for example, 71 percent of blacks over nine years of age were employed compared with 51 percent for whites.[14] Chinese were discriminated against, but they were employed building the railroads of the West. Neither phenomenon can be explained by racial likes or dislikes. The willingness to work for lower wages explains both.

The notion that it is sometimes necessary for some individuals to lower their price in order that some transactions can occur is offensive to the sensibilities of many people. These people support the minimum wage law as a matter of moral conviction motivated by concern for equity in the distribution of wealth. However, white racists' unions in South Africa have also been supporters of minimum wage laws and equal-pay-for-equal-work laws for blacks. The *New York Times* reported that in South Africa, where the racial climate is perhaps the most hostile in the world:

> Right wing white unions in the building trades have complained to the South African government that laws reserving skilled jobs for whites have [been] broken and should be abandoned in favor of equal-pay-for-equal-work laws. . . . The conservative building trades made it clear that they were not motivated by concern for black workers but had come to feel that legal job reservation had been so eroded by government exemptions that it no longer protected the white worker.[15]

To understand how job reservation laws became eroded requires only two bits of information: (1) During the post–World War II period, there was a significant building boom in South Africa, and (2) black construction workers were willing to accept wages of less than 25 percent of wages paid to white construction workers. Such a differential made racial discrimination in hiring a costly proposition. Firms that chose to hire whites instead of blacks paid dearly—$1.91

per hour versus $.39 per hour. White racist unions well rec-
ognized that equal-pay-for-equal-work laws (a variant of
minimum wage laws) would lower the cost of racial discrimination and thus improve their competitive position in the
labor market.

Moral philosophers can get into unending debate over
whether it is fair for some people to have to pay higher
prices for what they buy than others and accept lower prices
for what they sell (as in the case of labor services) than
others do. But solid economic evidence shows that whatever
the handicap, preventing people from lowering (raising) the
price of what they sell (buy) tends to reinforce that handicap.

U.S. Union Support for Minimum Wage Laws

As is the case in South Africa and elsewhere, unions in the
United States are also the major supporters of the minimum
wage law. While our unions have different stated intentions
behind their support of minimum wage laws, one must always remember that the *effect* of policy is by no means necessarily determined by the *intents* of policy. But a good case
can be made that the effects of the minimum wage law (high
unemployment among low-skilled workers) are its intentions. This can be readily understood if we consider as economists do that for many productive activities low-skilled
workers are substitutes for higher-skilled workers. And if
high-skilled workers, through organizing, can reduce or
eliminate the use of low-skilled workers, they achieve monopoly power and command higher wages. A numerical example can demonstrate the strategy.

Suppose a fence can be produced by using either *one*
high-skilled worker or by using *three* low-skilled workers.
If the wage of high-skilled workers is $38 per day, and that
of a low-skilled worker is $13 per day, the firm would employ
the high-skilled worker because costs would be less and profits higher ($38 versus $39). The high-skilled worker would
soon recognize that one of the ways to increase his wealth

would be to advocate a minimum wage of, say, $20 per day in the fencing industry. The arguments that the high-skilled worker would use to gain political support would be those given by any of our union leaders: "to raise the standard of living," "prevention of worker exploitation," "worker equality," and so forth. After the enactment of the minimum wage laws, the high-skilled worker can now demand any wage up to $60 per day (what it would now cost to hire three low-skilled workers) and retain employment.[16] Prior to the enactment of the minimum wage of $20 per day, a demand for $60 per day would have cost the high-skilled worker his job. Thus the effect of the minimum wage is to price the high-skilled worker's competition out of the market.

Whether the example given here accurately describes the motives of labor unions' support of and expenditures made lobbying for minimum wages is not really at issue. The effects of union action do not depend on its motivation. That is, whether the union means to help or to harm the low-skilled worker, the effect is to price him out of the market. However, it is worthwhile to note that the restrictive activities promoted by unions do reduce employment opportunities and the income of those forced out of the market. This fact suggests that union strategies to raise wages of their members must be complemented by their lobbying for government welfare programs. The reason is that if not having a job meant not eating, there would be considerable political disruption. Therefore, unions have incentives to support subsidy programs for those denied job access.[17] Thus, it is very probable that unions will lead the support for income subsidy programs such as Job Corps, summer work programs, CETA, food stamps, public service employment and welfare. The redistribution of income really constitutes a subsidy from society at large, who pay the taxes, to those who have used the various powers of government to restrict or eliminate job opportunity. Income subsidy programs have disguised the true effects of restriction created by unions and other economic agents by casting a few crumbs to those denied jobs in order to keep them quiet, thereby creating a permanent welfare class.

U.S. Business Support for Minimum Wage Laws

Businesses have sought protection from competition by way of the minimum wage law. President John Kennedy, when he was senator, supported increases in the minimum wage law as a way of protecting New England industry from competition with southern industry.[18] Farmers have supported agricultural minimum wage laws in order to reduce competition. A particularly insightful comment was made by Congressman Joseph Y. Resnick:

> Mr. Chairman, I would like to point out to all the members of the Northeast and from the city what this legislation means to them. For one thing, Mr. Chairman, it means that the farmers of the Northeast can compete fairly with farmers from the rest of the country.
>
> Now, Mr. Chairman, we have poultry farmers in our part of the country. Our farmers pay anywhere from $1.25 to $1.75 an hour for help. I ask you how can they compete with poultry farmers in Mississippi who pay $3 a day for a ten-hour day.[19]

There are numerous examples of business interests that are served by minimum wages. Surely included among them are businessmen's past interest in having U.S. minimum wage laws applied to U.S. territories and Puerto Rico. The underlying drive of businessmen, in their support for the minimum wage law, was to reduce competition that they would face from lower-wage areas. The minimum wage law gets very little political support from the low-wage states, mostly in the South.

Labor Market Myths

Before ending this chapter we should comment on several widely accepted labor market myths.

1. *If teenagers are allowed to work at subminimum wages, they will be employed while their parents go unemployed.* This statement is an example of what economists call the "lump of labor fallacy." The statement assumes that there is a finite number of jobs available whereby the acqui-

sition of one job by one person of necessity means that another person will lose his job. There is no evidence to support such a contention. The number of people holding jobs grew from less than a million during colonial times to nearly 100 million holding jobs now. All evidence suggests that this trend will continue. While there may be some substitutions, the overwhelming effect of subminimum wages would be to increase employment.

2. *The employment problem faced by youths and others is that there are simply no jobs available.* If this myth is accepted at face value, it is the same thing as saying that all human wants have been satisfied. In other words, it asserts that no one anywhere wishes to have more of some good or service. Again, there is no evidence to support such a claim. The quantity of labor employed, just as any other thing of value, conforms to the law of demand: the higher its price the less it is used, and vice versa. What people mean by this *particular* statement is that at some particular wage there are no jobs available. Nothing is strange about this observation, because at some particular wage anyone will find that his labor is not demanded. For example, if a writer informed his employer that the minimum wage that he was willing to work for was $200,000 per year, there would simply be no job available. This notion applies to any worker. The only difference is that the wage that would cause some people to be unemployed is higher than that which would cause other people to be unemployed.

3. *Many people are unemployed because they are low-skilled and have few qualifications.* Low skills explain low wages, but low skills cannot explain unemployment. A person is qualified or unqualified only in a relative sense—relative to some wage. To speak of qualifications or skills in an absolute sense has little meaning. For example, a carpenter who is qualified, and hence employable at a wage of $4 per hour, may be unqualified, and hence unemployable, at a wage of $10 per hour. This idea applies to anything. A Sears suit is "unqualified" to sell for the same price as a tailored Pierre Cardin suit.

One of the interesting aspects of skills and qualifications

is that if an organization of, say, carpenters can through legal institutions require that employers pay all carpenters hired a wage of $10 per hour, then they have artificially disqualified and made unemployable the carpenter who was formerly qualified and employable at the wage of $4 per hour.

This kind of artificial disqualification has direct application to the problems that minorities face in the labor market. Frequently, it is said that minorities have a high unemployment rate because of their low skills. How does one reconcile this statement with the fact that in earlier times minorities had lower unemployment rates? No one, we think, would be prepared to argue that blacks during earlier times had more education and training than blacks in present times and that is why they had higher employment rates. No, the real reason is that through the political mechanism (perhaps without intent) many blacks have been artificially disqualified.

4. *High youth unemployment reflects the "baby boom" of the post–World War II era.* This myth reflects a misunderstanding of the basic laws of supply and demand. Given a demand, an increased supply of labor (or for that matter anything else) results in lower prices in a free market. It just happens that the labor market in the United States is not free.

5. *Widespread automation is the cause of high unemployment rates among a large sector of the labor force.* This myth reflects both a kind of amnesia and the lump of labor fallacy. First, higher wages are the proximate cause of automation. When wages rise relative to capital costs, firms have incentives to substitute capital for labor. For example, when elevator operators negotiated a higher wage, a few years later we saw widespread installation of automatic elevators. After tomato pickers were brought under the minimum wage, we saw the implementation of tomato-picking machines. As grape pickers negotiate higher wages, we are now seeing the transition to grape-picking machines. Second, this myth is the lump of labor fallacy because it asserts that society has no use for the labor displaced by automation.

6. *The minimum wage law will give workers increased purchasing power that will sustain high employment.* This myth assumes that workers keep their jobs and work the same number of hours as before. Some workers will and some will not. The workers who lose their jobs as a result of a hypothetical right to earn $3.35 will find that the hypothetical right will not buy them groceries and housing. Furthermore, more wages are not necessarily the same thing as more purchasing power when the artificial wage increases give rise to political forces for inflation.

7. *The minimum wage law is an antipoverty weapon.* If this were true, we would have an instant solution to the world's poverty and underdevelopment problems. We would just advise countries to raise their minimum wage. The sad fact of business is that low-skilled workers are not so much underpaid as they are underskilled. The way to help them, as well as poor countries, is to make them more productive. This cannot be done with a stroke of the legislative pen.

These labor market myths have maintained their popularity down through the ages primarily because they have served particular interest groups and because many other people are decent and have legitimate concern for their fellowman. However, truly compassionate policy requires dispassionate analysis. Therefore, the debunking of these and other labor market myths is an important ingredient toward that end.

The minimum wage law, as well as many other laws that have placed minimum prices on labor transactions, has imposed incalculable harm on the most disadvantaged members of our society. The absence of work opportunities for many youngsters does not mean only an absence of pocket money. Early work opportunities provide much more than that. Early work opportunities teach youngsters how to find a job. They learn work attitudes. They learn the importance of punctuality and respect for supervision. These things learned in *any* job make a person a more valuable worker in the future. Furthermore, early work experiences give youngsters the pride and self-respect that comes from being financially independent. All the benefits of early work experiences are even more important for black youngsters who go to the nation's worst schools. If they are to learn something that will make them more valuable in the future, they have to learn it in the job market.

Since the minimum wage law does incalculable harm to the nation's youth, the only moral thing to do is repeal it. Failing that, a national subminimum wage would be a partial solution.

Invisible Victims

Some of the political support for the minimum wage reflects self-interest. It is a way to eliminate, as we have discussed, low wage competition. Others lend political support to minimum wage legislation because of a real concern for the disadvantaged worker. They think that the poor are helped to live a better life. In one sense these people are correct. The less poor are made better off and the poorest poor are made worse off. But the truly concerned supporter of the minimum wage law cannot see this.

The reason that this effect of the minimum wage law goes unnoticed is that there are policy blind spots. Very often the victims of many forms of social policy are invisible. They are not seen or accounted for by the do-gooders.

Do-gooders may see people working under "sweatshop" conditions. Old ladies working ten hours a day and earning $1.50 an hour. Or teenagers working well into the night for $1 an hour. Having made such an observation, the do-gooders may force the U.S. Department of Labor to do something about these conditions. The Labor Department may very well do something that may include heavy penalties on the factory owner for violations of wage laws and other labor laws.

Having brought this action, the do-gooders walk away triumphantly, knowing that good has won over evil. Six months later they may return to the factory. The people that they *see* are better off. They are earning the minimum wage and have better working conditions. Once again the do-gooders feel a sense of triumph.

What they do not see are the people, the old lady and kids, who no longer have a job. The old lady is without income and the kid may be standing on street corners committing crime. These are the invisible victims of the do-gooders' actions. Often the causes are invisible to the victims themselves: they do not know why they cannot find a job.

What the do-gooders forgot to ask before they enacted their policy to "help" is why would anyone work ten hours per day for the paltry sum of a dollar or two an hour? Would he have selected such a job if he had a better opportunity? Therefore, the "sweatshop" job was his best-known opportunity. Such a person is indeed unfortunate, but is he helped by the destruction of his best opportunity with the do-gooder offering him no replacement other than the dole?

The real problem, both in the U.S. and other countries, is that people are not so much underpaid as they are underskilled. The real task is to make skilled those people who are underskilled. This is not done by merely declaring, "As of January 1, 1981, everybody's productive output is now worth $3.35 per hour." This makes about as much sense, and accomplishes about as much, as doctors curing patients by merely declaring that they are cured.

CHAPTER 4

What Do Differences in Median Income Mean?

The great tragedy of Science—the slaying of a
beautiful hypothesis by an ugly fact.

—T. H. Huxley

Biogenesis and Abiogenesis

THERE ARE SIGNIFICANT INCOME DIFFERENCES by race. Social
scientists have searched for well over a decade for the answer. The statistic shrouded in mystery is the fact that black
median income is roughly 60 percent of white median income. In the 1960s, everyone was quite sure of the cause
of white/black income differences. It was racial discrimination. In the wake of legal litigation, antidiscriminatory laws
and affirmative action, now the question is why do these
differentials remain.

To examine the labor market for *current* racial discrimination is a very difficult statistical task. The statistician
must be able to compare likes with likes. This means that
he must discover all those human characteristics that have
some bearing on earning capacity. Some of these are quantifiable, such as age, years of schooling and experience. Other
influences are less quantifiable, such as quality of schooling,
mannerisms and demeanor and just plain luck. Somehow
the statisticians must standardize these variables to see how
much bearing the race of the individual has on his income.
Typically, the statistician/researcher concludes that after
controlling for all other differences, the remaining differ-

ence in income can be accounted for by racial discrimination. Such an approach, though none better is known, is fraught with many technical difficulties. These difficulties include inadequate measures of employee productivity and inclusiveness of all the income-relevant variables and variable quantification. But for whatever it's worth, where economists have been able to do a good job in handling these problems, very little *current* labor market discrimination exists.[1]

This chapter will focus on one area of the labor market for analysis. Definitive answers will not be provided. But questions to "sure" answers will be asked. The discussion focuses on comparisons between black and white professionals. Though professional occupations constitute only a small fraction of the total labor market, there are some interesting facts uncovered that might offer insight into the labor market in general.

A widely noted characteristic of median income differences between black and white workers is the fact that they spread as black education increases. The following statement is typical of what has acquired axiomatic status in the racial discrimination literature:

> Another reason for arguing that racial discrimination exists in the demand for labor is that the measured income differentials are greater at higher educational levels. For example, among males aged 35 to 44 in the northern United States in 1959, the ratio of mean non-white to mean white income was 79 percent for those with elementary school education, 70 percent for those with high school education and only 59 percent for those with college education . . . it is hard to give any explanation for these figures based on supply considerations. It is most reasonable to explain them on the hypothesis of a racial discrimination in demand that is more intensive for higher economic positions, the jobs into which the more educated go.[2]

And, as Finis Welch reports:

> The most important result is that the market evidently discriminates much more heavily against a Negro's education

than against his skilled labor. Thus, relative to whites with similar schooling, Negro income declines as school completion increases.[3]

Numerous statistical studies have been motivated by these and similar findings. By and large, the studies conclude that after controlling for education and other socioeconomic variables *thought* to influence earnings, there remains an "unexplained residual" in the comparison of black/white earnings. The "unexplained residual" is said to be racial discrimination in the labor force. The typical explanation given for the unexplained residual is that employers or employees exhibit a distaste for working with blacks. Therefore, if the black worker is to be employed, he must offer a compensating difference in the form of lower earnings to offset white employer/employee distastes. The explanation goes on to assert that the distaste for blacks is greater at higher-level jobs since high-level jobs entail more supervisory responsibilities and whites have an aversion to having a black supervisor. This is said to make the highly educated black less valuable to the firm.

The racial taste hypothesis of earning differentials between black and white workers can be satisfactory only if there is confidence that *all* variables that influence income are known and adequately controlled. However, there are many factors that can influence income and productivity which are statistically elusive. Some of the more difficult variables to account for in statistical analysis but known to influence productivity are chance, genetic endowment and household or cultural values that shape individual future versus present choices (and hence educational investment decisions), just to name a few. But ignoring these difficulties for the moment, let us look at some facts.

One of the best-kept secrets of all times and virtually totally ignored in the literature on racial differences in earnings is that black/white female professional income ratios do not exhibit patterns even remotely similar to their male counterparts. Table 4 presents these facts. In 1960, black male college graduates earned a median income which was only 60 percent of white male college graduates. This is compared to black female college graduates whose median income was 102 percent of that of white female college graduates. Black female college graduates earned a median income that was 2 percent higher than their white female counterparts. Table 4 also shows that for black female high school and grade school graduates, median earnings were significantly closer to those of white females than black males' earnings were to those of their counterparts.

Table 4
Ratio of Black/White Income by Skill Levels in 1960

EDUCATION	MALE	FEMALE
College	.60	1.02
High School	.69	.79
Grade School	.75	.87

SOURCE: Richard B. Freeman, "Labor Market Discrimination," in Michael D. Intriligator and David A. Kendrick (eds.), *Frontiers of Quantitative Economics,* vol. II (New York: American Elsevier Publishing Co., 1974), p. 503.

The story does not end there; more remarkable results were found in the 1970 census. By 1970, the median earnings of black male college graduates rose from 60 to 73 percent of similar whites, while in the same year, blacks classified as professionals earned 72 percent of the income of white male professionals. More evidence of racial discrimination? What about black and white females? It turns out that in 1970, black female college graduates earned an income which was 125 percent of their white counterparts! Those classified as professionals earned incomes of 118 percent of their white counterparts! That is, black female college graduates and professionals, compared to their white counterparts, were respectively earning 25 and 18 percent more![4]

It is easy to suggest that the favorable status of black female professionals is due to affirmative action and civil rights legislation. But the economic position of black female

Female Black/White Income Ratios by Region for Ages 14 and Over, 1950, 1960, 1970

	1950	1960	1970
Northeast	.84	.99	1.17
North Central	.86	.97	1.17
South	.58	.56	.67
West	.86	.96	1.08

SOURCE: U.S. Census of Population 1950, 1960, 1970

college graduates relative to whites is not a new phenomenon. As early as 1950, black female college graduates earned a median income that was 91 percent that of white female college graduates.[5] The fact of business is that on the whole the difference between median incomes for black and white females in the general work force have been considerably less than that of males. Table 5 gives black/white female income ratios by region for females 14 years of age and over in the years 1950, 1960 and 1970. Table 6 gives the same information for males 14 years of age and over.

Table 5 shows that, except for the South, black females achieved economic parity with white females by 1970. Moreover, the data show that black females as a group, except for the South, have had median incomes quite close to that of white females for nearly three decades. Black males are

Table 6
Male Black/White Income Ratios by Region for Ages 14 and Over, 1950, 1960, 1970

	1950	1960	1970
Northeast	.75	.71	.75
North Central	.81	.76	.79
South	.58	.56	.56
West	.68	.71	.71

SOURCE: U.S. Census of Population 1950, 1960, 1970

just now achieving the economic position relative to white males that black females, relative to white females, had achieved by 1950!

The presence of these facts seriously calls into question most theories of racial earnings differentials, particularly the *relative discrimination* hypothesis where it is argued by Welch, for example, that discrimination is against black education.[6] The reason to question this is that the relative discrimination hypothesis fails to explain why black females relative to white females appear not to be discriminated against. Are they immune? Using the identical reasoning utilized by Welch and others, the argument could be produced, as far as female college graduates are concerned, that there is *racial discrimination against white female college graduates.* This, according to the prevailing thought, would be the only way that we could explain the fact that black female college graduates earn higher wages than their white counterparts.[7]

Therefore, as suggested by the discussion so far, there are at least three important questions that are inadequately answered in the racial discrimination literature: (1) Why do black/white female income ratios rise with increased education while the opposite is the case with black/white male median income ratio; (2) Why is it that black/white female income differences are virtually nonexistent, as a group, while there are significant differences between black and white males; and (3) What can possibly explain why the median income of the black female professional is 25 percent higher than that of white female professionals?

Definitive answers to these questions are all but impossible because of the highly aggregated form of data that are available. That is, it appears to be meaningless to use aggregated data such as the median income of persons to explain a behavior phenomenon that is essentially at the unit level of analysis. To say more-meaningful things about racial discrimination, one needs to have wage/race and other data by occupation by firm. Such a source of data is unknown to the writer.

However, there are some things that can be done with

census data which, while not providing complete answers, tend to weaken some of the usual explanations given for black/white income differences. The standard explanations range from poor quality education and lower group socioeconomic status to labor market racial discrimination. If these factors cause black male income to be significantly lower than that of white males, then why is it that black females, who presumably share the same environmental background as do black males, have incomes that are for the most part *equal* to or greater than white females?

Some insight into these questions may be found if we analyze the racial differences (or the lack thereof) in the professional occupational distribution broken down by sex. The specific question that is asked is how do blacks and whites compare, by sex, within the professional category of jobs? The reasoning behind this question is that: (1) If occupational distributions are similar, by race, within a sex group, then preliminarily we may attach more significance to the wage discrimination hypothesis of racial median income differences; (2) If the occupational distribution differs by race within a sex group, then one possible explanation of racial income differences may reflect that one group may be more highly represented in the lower-paying jobs within the professional ranks.

To examine differences and similarities between black and white professionals by race, the 1970 *Census of Population* was used. Tables 7 and 8 are representations of the census of professionals broken down into 27 professional classes. To test for the degree of similarity in the occupational distributions, the Kendall rank order coefficient of correlation was used.[8] This is a statistical test for comparison. The closer the coefficient is to 1.0, the more similar the groups under comparison. The coefficient for black and white professional males was (.68) and that for black and white females was (.85). A coefficient of (1.0) would suggest that the distributions were identical. The fact that the coefficient is significantly higher in the case of black/white females is interpreted as meaning that the similarity in distribution among professional occupations is stronger in the

Table 7
Racial/Sexual Distribution of Occupations, Male

	WHITE MALES	% OF TOTAL WHITE MALE PROFESSIONALS	RANKING ORDER FOR WHITE MALES	BLACK MALES	% OF TOTAL BLACK MALE PROFESSIONALS	RANKING ORDER FOR BLACK MALES
Professional Technicians	6,394,050			237,293		
Accounting	500,302	.078	5	9,026	.04	10
Architects	51,545	.008	20	1,151	.005	22
Computer Specialists	194,261	.03	11	5,803	.02	14
Engineers	1,140,035	.18	1	12,995	.05	6
Farm Management Advisors	5,982	.0009	26	337	.001	26
Foresters & Conservationists	36,977	.005	23	638	.003	25
Home Management Advisors	186	.00005	27	16	.00007	27
Lawyers & Judges	252,219	.04	9	3,231	.01	17
Life & Physical Scientists	167,063	.027	13	4,845	.02	15
Operations & Systems Research	69,428	.01	18	1,112	.005	23
Personnel & Labor Relations	188,314	.03	12	8,337	.04	11
Doctors, Dentists, etc.	470,476	.07	6	9,581	.04	8
Nurses, Dieticians	44,126	.007	22	6,808	.02	13
Health Technologists	66,872	.01	19	8,007	.03	12
Religious Workers	211,521	.03	10	12,840	.05	7
Social Scientists	83,760	.01	16	2,013	.008	20
Social Workers	89,602	.01	15	15,013	.06	5
Teachers (University)	331,224	.05	7	9,211	.04	9

Librarians	24,676	.004	24	1,412	.006	21
Mathematical Specialists	21,984	.003	25	643	.003	24
Teachers (Non-University)	745,673	.12	2	50,891	.21	1
Engineering Technicians	670,054	.10	3	21,836	.09	3
Technicians (Nonhealth, Eng.)	131,023	.02	14	2,993	.01	18
Vocational & Education Counselors	54,133	.008	21	4,414	.02	16
Writers, Artists, Entertainers	491,756	.08	4	18,236	.08	4
Research Workers	82,023	.01	17	1,999	.008	19
Professional Workers (Allocated)	258,830	.04	8	23,908	.10	2

SOURCE: U.S. Bureau of the Census, *Census of Population: 1970 Characteristics of the Population*, vol. I, pt. I, United States Summary, sec. 2 (Washington D.C.: Government Printing Office, 1973).

Table 8
Racial/Sexual Distribution of Occupations, Female

	WHITE FEMALES	% OF TOTAL WHITE FEMALE PROFESSIONALS	RANKING ORDER FOR WHITE FEMALES	BLACK FEMALES	% OF TOTAL BLACK FEMALE PROFESSIONALS	RANKING ORDER FOR BLACK FEMALES
Professional Technicians	4,181,932			374,041		
Accounting	171,565	.04	5	7,495	.02	7
Architects	1,789	.0004	25	107	.0003	26
Computer Specialists	46,360	.01	13	2,655	.007	13
Engineers	18,465	.004	19	684	.002	22
Farm Management Advisors	1,096	.0003	27	131	.0004	25
Foresters & Conservationists	1,491	.0004	26	89	.0002	27
Home Management Advisors	4,498	.001	24	618	.002	21
Lawyers & Judges	12,478	.003	21	497	.001	23
Life & Physical Scientists	24,444	.006	16	1,486	.004	15
Operations & Systems Research	7,073	.002	23	443	.001	24
Personnel & Labor Relations	80,844	.02	10	6,276	.02	10
Doctors, Dentists, etc.	42,378	.02	11	1,855	.005	14
Nurses, Dieticians	803,976	.19	2	69,620	.18	2
Health Technologists	159,175	.04	6	16,151	.04	5
Religious Workers	24,210	.006	17	1,031	.003	19
Social Scientists	19,391	.005	18	1,075	.003	18
Social Workers	124,604	.03	8	25,778	.06	4
Teachers (University)	127,305	.03	7	7,599	.02	6
Librarians	93,660	.02	9	6,808	.02	8
Math Specialists	11,147	.003	22	737	.002	20
Teachers (Non-University)	1,719,739	.41	1	172,372	.46	1
Engineering Technicians	80,375	.02	12	4,820	.01	12
Technicians (Nonhealth, Eng.)	15,977	.004	20	1,075	.003	17

Vocational & Education Counselors	40,263	.01	14	5,469	.01	11
Writers, Artists, & Entertainers	214,809	.05	3	6,643	.02	9
Research Workers	28,186	.007	15	1,284	.003	16
Professional Workers (Allocated)	206,534	.05	4	31,243	.08	3

SOURCE: U.S. Bureau of the Census, *Census of Population: 1970 Characteristics of the Population*, vol. I, pt. I, United States Summary, sec. 2 (Washington, D.C.: U.S. Government Printing Office, 1973).

case of black and white females than in the case of their male counterparts.

These findings suggest that a good part of the income differential between white and black male professionals may lie in occupational distribution differences between the two populations. This would imply that *even if* white and black males were paid identical incomes within an occupation, significant differences would occur when measuring median professional income. For example, the largest category (rank 1) of white male professionals are classed as engineers. This class constitutes 18 percent of white male professionals. On the other hand, only 5 percent of black male professionals are classed as engineers—rank 6 among black male professionals. Non-university teachers is the largest group for black professionals (21 percent) while only 12 percent of white male professionals are so classified.

The significance of these occupational differences is seen when we compare median earnings in these occupations. According to the 1970 Census, the median earnings of engineers was $13,149! The median earnings for non-university teachers was $8,711! Making the most heroic assumption that blacks and whites earn the same pay within the respective occupations, there would be significant differences in black and white male professional incomes at the median. However, the fact of business is that there are differences. The median earnings of black male engineers was $10,494 compared to $13,149 for white males, while the earnings of black male non-university teachers was $7,777 and that of white male non-university teachers was $8,711. On the other hand, median earnings for black female non-university teachers, $6,620, exceeded that of white female non-university teachers, $6,369.

For female professionals, there is an entirely different story. Non-university teaching is the largest category (rank 1) for both black and white female professionals. Forty-six percent of black female and 41 percent of white female professionals are in that category. Nurses and dieticians are the second most important category among female professionals. Eighteen percent of black and 19 percent of white professionals are nurses and dieticians. Table 8 shows the rank order for black and white female professionals which shows that black/white female professions are far more similar in their distribution across the professional occupational structure than are black/white male professionals.

Why black male professionals differ so significantly from their white counterparts, and black female professionals do not, is a matter for interesting speculation.

A more interesting question is, Given the similarities between black and white female professionals, why is it that the median income for black female professionals is 125 percent that of white female professionals? One thing that is implied by the showing of black females is that sex discrimination is not compounded by race discrimination. The higher earnings of black female professionals could show the effect of rural versus nonrural employment and compensation. Blacks, as a group, are more urban than are whites as a group.[9] To the extent that urban salaries are higher than rural salaries, the fact that a larger percentage of black female professionals are urban, this coupled with the fact that their professional occupation distribution is very similar to white, could very well account for the income differential. Particularly so, when we take note of the fact that teachers and nurses, the most important category of employment for women, earn higher salaries in metropolitan areas than in nonmetropolitan areas.

Income differences can be the result of factors other than racial discrimination by employers. They could be the result of factors having little or nothing to do with discrimination. Factors racially benign such as age, geography, educational attainment, family size and personal occupational choice can account for the results we see.[10] But income differences can be explained by racial discrimination either by employers or other agents in the society. The policy-relevant question is how much of a role does racial discrimination play and how much of a role do the other factors play in explaining white/black differences in income? To develop effective policy requires correct identification of causal relationships.

CHAPTER 5

Occupational and Business Licensing

People of the same trade seldom meet together, even for merriment and diversion, but the conversation ends in a conspiracy against the public, or in some other contrivance to raise prices.

—Adam Smith
  Wealth of Nations

FEDERAL, STATE AND LOCAL GOVERNMENTS regulate the conditions by which individuals may enter and conduct themselves in many businesses and occupations.[1] The often stated justification for government regulation is the desire to protect public safety and morals, provide for orderly markets, eliminate unscrupulous practitioners and provide for a fair rate of return. Apart from the "public spirited" *intentions* that may underlie the regulation of businesses and occupations, there are the *effects* of regulation that can be analyzed through economic analysis. It is not required in any way that in order to analyze effects of regulation we analyze, deny or even acknowledge its intents.[2] The emphasis here is that intentions are one part of social legislation and effects of social legislation are another part since such intentions of policy may bear no relation to policy results.

Entry into a number of businesses and occupations is controlled at the various levels of government. For example, entry into interstate trucking is controlled by the U.S. Interstate Commerce Commission while *intra*state trucking is controlled at the state level, usually by some public utility authority. In some states, entry into the taxi business is con-

trolled by a state authority and in other states the responsi-
bility is delegated to the municipalities. Adding to the com-
plexity of business and occupational regulation is that they
are strictly controlled in some states and municipalities
while in others there may be little or no control.

The control by government over the entry into an occupation is typically done through licensure laws. People who
practice the trade without being licensed are subject to criminal prosecution which includes arrest, fines or imprisonment. Licensure laws have various legal minimum requirements that must be satisfactorily met as a condition of entry.
These may include: prior minimum schooling, citizenship,
written, oral or practical competency testing, attendance at
"approved" schools or "approved" apprenticeship programs,
prior occupational experience, minimum age requirements,
and so forth.

Licensing laws are administered by experts who are selected from those who are already practicing the occupation
or business.[3] These experts, sometimes called commission-
ers, change and modify licensure laws. They have full state
police powers at their disposal to enforce concurrence and
compliance among practitioners.

The economic effects of occupational and business licensure are quite predictable. The most immediate effect of
licensing is that the number of practitioners is smaller than
it would otherwise be. The reasons are mostly the result
of higher entry costs for the licensed activity. Some licenses
require many months of schooling as in the cases of cosmeti-
cians and barbers. Others require installation of costly
health and safety equipment. Yet others require the purchase of the license or "certificate of authorization" which
can cost into the millions of dollars. Then some licensing
jurisdictions issue only a fixed number of licenses or authori-
zations. All of these licensure requirements raise the cost
of entry, which leads necessarily to a smaller number of
practitioners in the licensed activity.

Fewer practitioners is the primary effect of licensing.
The secondary effect is that the price of the good or service
is higher than it would otherwise be. Therefore, the effect
of restricting entry to a business or occupation, and fre-

quently the unstated intent of licensing, is to raise the incomes of incumbent practitioners. Informal evidence seems to support this: (1) most licensure laws are the result of intense lobbying by incumbent practitioners, *not* consumers demanding better protection; (2) when incumbents in an unlicensed trade lobby for licensing (or when incumbents in an already licensed trade lobby for higher entry requirements) they virtually always seek a grandfather's clause that exempts them from meeting all the requirements; (3) violations of the licensing codes by practitioners, such as price cutting and extra hours, are nearly always reported to the licensing board by the incumbent practitioners and *not* by customers.[4]

The severest form of occupational licensing is that which imposes a *fixed* number of licensed practitioners *in addition to education, age, citizenship and apprenticeship requirements*. Numerical limits tend to produce the highest economic rewards for those already in the trade.[5] For the most part, legal restrictions on the number of practitioners in *occupations* are not often set by statute. The right to set and modify the number of practitioners is effectively done by unions or trade associations. Unions accomplish this through their power to set the number of apprenticeship "openings" or restrict union membership "openings" or use a probationary status to adjust to transitory changes in demand for the services of their members. Licensing arrangements, in general, restrict entry by raising entry cost and not so much by imposing numerical limits on the number of practitioners. The reason appears to be mostly political. It is a far more successful political strategy to argue for practitioners of a trade to justify higher entry costs on the ground that it raises standards and hence consumers are protected against quacks. Such pleas can be made under the pretense of public interest. It is considerably more difficult to argue public interest by simply restricting the number of practitioners. Numerical restrictions must be argued on the ground of adverse "third party" effects, such as too many taverns will lead to drunkenness or too many taxis will lead to congestion. The liquor industry and the taxicab industry, incidentally, are two of many areas of business

licensing where many municipalities impose numerical restrictions on practitioners.

In some occupations the state permission to practice the
trade is transferable. The original owner of the license can
transfer it to another person. Hence the license commands
a market price. The taxicab industry, the retail liquor business and the trucking business are examples of businesses
where the license is transferable. Where licenses are sold
on the market, this affords the opportunity to calculate the
value to practitioners to do business in a state-monopolized
market. The selling price of the license represents the dis-
counted value of having the right to earn monopoly income
over the life of the business. For example, the market price
of a license to own and operate a *single* taxicab on the streets
of New York has been approximately $60,000. *If* entry were
open to all would-be taxicab owners, the amount of money
that people would be willing to pay for the taxi license would
be zero. Taxi owners' earnings would be equal to the costs
of providing taxi services. Taxi prices would be equal to
the cost of providing that service (prices lower than those
that now exist). However, a numerical limit on the number
of taxis produces abnormal profits and hence the willingness
of people to pay the license price. In other words, people
are willing to pay $60,000 for a taxi license because they
expect to earn higher-than-normal profits. In the case of
New York, there have been no new licenses issued since
the early pre-World War II period. On the other hand, personal incomes have risen creating a higher demand for taxi
service. Most of the adjustment to the higher demand has
taken the form of higher prices for taxi services. If there
had been open opportunities, the long-run adjustment would
have been in the form of *more* taxis and perhaps a price
increase but not as high as that that now exists. The next
chapter will more fully explore the taxi industry.

Racial Effects of Occupational and Business Licensing

In addition to the effects of licensure already outlined, there
are others. The major effect of licensing is that it leads to

fewer practitioners than would be the case in the absence of licensing. This, of course, means that there are fewer employment opportunities, and hence income-earning opportunities. Occupational or business licensing has also significant effects on the distribution of income. The distributional effects of licensing are not equally shared among the potential and actual market participants.

Occupational licensing raises entry costs through various requirements, thereby causing some potential entrants to decide against pursuing the occupation. This category of requirements are age, minimum secondary school education, citizenship and license fees. No person is explicitly rejected. People decide not to try in the first place. Obviously, these requirements are more burdensome to some demographic groups than others. For example, the possession of a high school diploma, as a preliminary requirement, will impose a greater burden on those demographic groups who experience a higher high school dropout rate.

A common form that many licensing examinations take is of two parts: a written part and a performance part. This introduces considerable bias and this is particularly so when the written portion is of little significance in predicting the presence of practical performance talents. This is because those with better education have greater facility with written expression. Potential entrants with limited reading ability and those whose native language is not English will be disadvantaged.

Often licensing requirements spell minimum hours of specialized education at "approved" schools. Schooling requirements involve tuition costs and, as such, exclusion on the basis of availability of financial resources will not be evenly spread across all demographic groups.

Stuart Dorsey studied the distributional effects of occupational licensing of cosmetologists (beauticians) in Missouri and Illinois.[6] He found that in both samples the black failure rate was two to three times that that would have been the case if race and failure rate were unrelated. In the Missouri sample only 3 percent of successful applicants are black while blacks constituted 21 percent of failures.

Similar results were obtained in the Illinois sample: 38 percent of failures were black applicants while only 11 percent of successful applicants were black. The Dorsey study further reported that black examination scores averaged more than ten points lower than whites when years of education and training are held constant.

Both Illinois and Missouri require that cosmetology applicants pass a performance test in addition to the written examination. On the performance examination the score is based upon the applicant's performance on a person that the applicant chooses as a model. All applicants, at the time they take the performance examination, are unaware of their score on the written portion. Dorsey reports that the total failure rate on the practical examination is low. In Missouri the failure rate was 13 percent and in Illinois it was 5 percent. But more remarkable than this finding is that the characteristics (race, education and apprenticeship) that are important in written examination performance have *no* explanatory value for the score on the practical examination. In other words, on the practical examination, *race has no statistical significance* with success as an explanatory variable.

Put straightforwardly, the written examination acts to exclude applicants, mainly by race, who are just as productive as others as evaluated by practical examination. The Dorsey study concludes that the occupational licensing of cosmetologists: (1) screens out people on the basis of characteristics unrelated to job performance; and (2) causes an overinvestment in education and formal training because much of the required training does not improve productivity and therefore is individually and socially wasteful. In addition, licensing serves to reinforce handicaps suffered by disadvantaged minorities.

Therefore, the theoretical predictions made by economists about the adverse racial effects of occupational licensure are borne out here by empirical evidence. Furthermore, the exclusion of disadvantaged people does not serve the public-interest arguments that are so often made for occupational licensing. When qualified people, as indicated by the practical performance tests, are denied entry because they failed the written test, the "public interest" is not enhanced. The consuming public is made worse off through higher prices and longer queues. The only clear beneficiaries of occupational licensing are incumbent practitioners who can charge higher prices and hence have higher incomes as a result of their monopolized market.

CHAPTER 6

The Taxicab Industry

"Give me your tired, your poor,
    Your huddled masses yearning to breathe free,
    The wretched refuse of your teeming shore,
Send these, the homeless, tempest-tossed, to me:
    I lift my lamp beside the golden door."

—Emma Lazarus
    "The New Colossus"

TAXICAB AND JITNEY OPERATIONS are two closely related business opportunities that lie within the capital and skills limitations of many urban poor.[1] Initial capital costs are modest when compared to other businesses. It is estimated that initial outlay, which includes a car, meter, radio and liability insurance would rarely exceed $5,000 for the operation of a single vehicle as a taxi. Furthermore, most of this outlay is recoverable if an owner defaults, thereby increasing the likelihood of bank finance. The personal business skills necessary to become a taxi owner-operator are similarly minimal. No more is required than the ability to operate a car and to learn locations in the city and its environs.

Despite the fact that the *real* entry conditions are minimal for the taxicab industry, there are significant, and for many insurmountable, politically erected barriers to entry. These barriers appear mostly in the form of local regulations that specify entry conditions. In all major American cities except three, the taxicab industry is a highly restricted government-regulated monopoly.[2] Some cities have restrictions on the number of taxicab licenses (permits or medallions) they issue. Other cities grant exclusive operating rights to one or more fleet operators. The city may allow only one fleet company to operate within its city limits. New York City is an example of the former which will be discussed in some detail because it is such an outstanding case.

New York Entry Restrictions

The municipal government of New York City requires a medallion for each taxicab operating in the city.[3] The code also provides for regulation of taxi fares and other conditions of operation. The medallion system began as a requirement of the Haas Act of 1937. Under the Haas Act, the city sold medallions for $10 to all persons *then* operating taxis in New York City. There were 13,566 original medallions issued, but 1,794 of the original medallions were returned to the city during World War II by their owners who went into the armed forces. Since 1937 no new medallions have been issued and the 1,794 turned into the city during World War II have not been reissued, leaving the city with 11,772 medallions, which in turn sets the upper limit on the number of taxis that may operate within the city. The owner of a medallion pays a small annual fee, but the medallion itself and the rights that it confers to the owner is private property. And as such it is transferable and commands a market price.

The selling price for a medallion for an independent taxi is now approximately $60,000.[4] The selling price of a medallion for a fleet taxi is $45,000. With 8,424 fleet taxi medallions and 3,348 independent taxi medallions, the estimated total market value of medallions in New York City is nearly $600 million. The artificially high entry cost means that if an individual wished to become an independent taxi owner-operator, the full cash cost of entry approaches $70,000. In practice, the initial outlay is less because some New York banks will lend up to $25,000 for a taxi medallion.[5]

These very high prices for taxi medallions can be readily explained economically. If the taxi industry were a free enterprise industry, namely, open to all potential entrants, the market value of a medallion would be zero. But to the extent that there is government-controlled entry, which confers monopoly power on incumbent taxi owners, and medallions are transferable, medallions will command a price. The present value (selling price) of the medallion represents and measures the value of the increased earnings that the taxi owner earns as a result of being able to sell taxi services in a government-protected monopoly market. In other words, the value of the medallion shows what the buyer is willing to pay for government protection from free market competition.[6]

Therefore, the medallion system of New York keeps the supply of taxis constant. The inevitable result of this is that when there is an increase in public demand for taxi services, as there has been in New York since 1937, there is no response in the form of more legal taxis. The response to the higher demand is mostly in the form of higher taxi fares and poorer-quality taxi service. This is the natural result of monopolized markets: the tendency of higher prices and lower-quality service when a seller is insulated from open market competition.

New York's Ghetto Response to the Taxi Monopoly

Several ghetto communities have responded to the medallioned taxicab monopoly and the grossly inferior services it provides to ghetto communities. In New York this response has taken the form of "gypsy" taxicabs. The emergence of gypsy (illegal) taxicabs is in part a direct response to the failure of the medallioned industry to provide an adequate level of taxi services. Ghettos such as Harlem, Bedford Stuyvesant, Brownsville and the South Bronx, to name a few neighborhoods in New York City, have consistently received poor taxi service from the medallioned industry. Many residents in these communities simply installed meters, painted signs and put lights on their private cars and declared them taxis and cruised the neighborhoods, providing taxi services.

High risks of robberies and other violence is the reason given by the medallioned taxi industry for not providing services in these communities. In addition, medallioned operators perceive these areas as being economically unprofitable compared to the central business district and some other areas of the city. To a significant degree, these claims are correct. One report estimates that 70 percent of all taxi robberies occur in black or Puerto Rican neighborhoods of the city.[7] As such, there is considerable inducement for many medallioned taxi drivers not to operate in these neighborhoods.

High crime and lower profitability have left an unmet demand for taxi services which has been taken up by illegal gypsy taxis. Estimates vary considerably on the size of the gypsy cab service in New York. The *New York Times* estimates that 4,000 to 5,000 such taxis operate in New York's ghettos.[8] Michael J. Lazar, the first chairman of the newly created Taxi and Limousine Commission, estimates that there are as many as 15,000 gypsy taxis operating in the city.[9] If the latter estimate is correct, the illegal taxi industry is numerically larger than the legal taxi industry, which consists of a maximum of 11,772 taxis.

Such a large illegal operation is possible for two reasons. One, because of poor services by the medallioned industry and two, because the authorities do not arrest gypsy taxi operators as long as their operations are limited to New York's ghettos. The Taxi and Limousine Commission, the courts and recent mayors have shown a similar reluctance to suppress illegal taxi operations. In no small part, this reluctance reflects official recognition of the poor services provided to the ghetto by the medallioned industry. However, when gypsy taxi drivers, emboldened by their ghetto success at ignoring the law, started to operate in the central business district and other nonghetto, higher income areas, they encountered resistance. Some of the resistance was in the form of violent attacks and the burning of gypsy taxis by the medallioned industry. Gypsy drivers, on the other hand, returned these actions in kind on many occasions. Another response to the bold action of the gypsies was that the Taxi and Limousine Commission started pressing for the enforcement of city taxi law. Also they took out full-page advertisements in local newspapers warning potential taxi patrons of the hazards of using unlicensed taxis.[10] The gypsy's penetration into the medallioned taxi market was made easier because their initial thrust came at a time when the Taxi and Limousine Commission granted a substantial increase in taxi fares which led to an increase in the willingness of New Yorkers to use gypsy taxis.

New York's gypsy taxi industry is a combination of illegal and semilegal operators. The semilegal component consists of private livery drivers. Private liveries are not licensed by the City of New York. They may operate as a vehicle for hire if they are licensed by the State of New York as an omnibus. But livery drivers are required by law to obtain *all* of their business either by telephone or by off-the-street requests for service. This distinction between private liveries and taxicabs has broken down in recent years. It is estimated that at least 75 percent of private livery business is obtained by passenger hails while cruising along the street. That is, private liveries conduct their business in a fashion reserved by law for medallioned taxis.[11]

There are no reliable figures on the racial composition of taxi owners and private livery drivers (and much less about gypsy taxis) because of prohibitions by the New York State Human Rights Commission. But according to one estimate, nearly 95 percent of all livery drivers are either black or Puerto Rican.[12] In telephone conversation with Joseph Basora of the Taxi and Limousine Commission, the writer was told that the racial composition of the illegal gypsy industry (private livery drivers who behave as taxis are considered gypsy by the Commission) is virtually black- and Puerto Rican–dominated.

The flourishing gypsy operation in New York is indicative of at least three important factors: (1) abnormal profits are currently being earned in New York's legal taxi industry. Simple economic theory makes the prediction that when above-average profits exist, the potential for entry also exists; (2) the fact that most of the entrants are black or Puerto Rican shows that these minorities *can,* with relative ease, provide a service that is socially valuable. Evidence that a socially valuable service is being provided is that patrons are willing to pay and the service has existed more than ten years; (3) the fact that the gypsy taxi service survives proves that these producers are capable of adapting to the environment and provide services that cannot be provided by the medallioned industry. The medallioned taxis allege that they cannot provide services to the ghetto because of high crime and unprofitability; somehow the gypsy operator can. Finally, and most importantly, the flourishing gypsy cab operation has significant implication for other areas of economic life. New York's blacks and Puerto Ricans obtained a chance to earn a livelihood providing taxi services by openly disregarding monopolistic laws. It so happens that the authorities in New York tacitly condone this illegal behavior. But there are many other areas of economic life where poor blacks and Puerto Ricans have the fitness requirements to compete on equal footing. But in these areas the monopoly barriers to entry are institutionally and legally enforced.

Philadelphia Taxi Industry

In Philadelphia, the taxicab industry is regulated by the Pennsylvania Public Utility Commission (PUC).[13] Taxicabs are specifically designated as common carriers and are issued a certificate of "public convenience and necessity." A certificate to own and operate a taxi in Philadelphia can be obtained from the PUC for the payment of $20 *provided* the applicant is deemed fit and he can prove the need for additional services. To prove "public convenience and necessity" is the most formidable aspect of the entry barrier. When an application for a certificate is made, the PUC permits all existing taxicab owners to protest the application of the prospective entrant. The city's incumbent taxi owners retain attorneys at the state capitol in Harrisburg for the *expressed* purpose of keeping new taxi owners out of the taxi business. By tying up certificate applicants in costly and lengthy court procedures, existing companies have discouraged entry and have gained monopoly control of the city's taxi industry.[14] The reason for limiting entry is that it protects the market value of certificates held by existing companies which now sell for approximately $20,000 (down from $35,000).

Taxicab regulation has brought about severe transportation consequences for Philadelphia. Philadelphia, a city of nearly 2 million people, has about 500 taxicabs in operation—down from approximately 1,300 taxis in 1961. Much of the decline is a result of the several bankruptcies of the city's largest fleet operator—the Yellow Cab Company. The number of taxis operated by the city's independent operators has remained constant at 175 vehicles over the period.

Despite this drastic decline in the number of taxis, the Public Utilities Commission, in the last forty years, has issued only a handful of new taxi certificates. Only recently, in March of 1979, did the Commission vote to award citywide operating rights to a taxi association that had formerly been excluded from citywide operation. This action was unsuccessfully contested by United and Yellow Cab Companies who had citywide operating rights as well as rights to operate in the area served by the company that had formerly been denied citywide rights.

There are no reliable estimates on the level of illegal taxicab operation in Philadelphia. According to one newspaper account, there are some 40 gypsy taxis that operate at Philadelphia's train stations, airport and bus stations.[15] In the poor neighborhoods of North Philadelphia, it is estimated that at least 25 gypsies operate ferrying shoppers to and from shopping centers. While the gypsy cab operation has grown in recent years, it does not compare in any way to that in New York.

The Pennsylvania Public Utility Commission is very lax about the enforcement of taxicab laws. They concede that there is not much that they can do about it because of legal rules of evidence. For the most part, they have only issued Letters of Warning to illegal taxi operators. According to Commission files, in 1977 there were sixteen Letters of Warning issued in Philadelphia and in 1978 there were only two such letters issued.[16]

The Taxicab Industry in Washington, D.C.

The taxicab industry in the nation's capitol differs markedly from that found in other major metropolitan areas. For all intents and purposes, there is *open* entry to Washington's taxicab industry. The regulatory agency, the Public Service Commission, controls tariffs and some other conditions of operation such as vehicle safety and insurance requirements. Taxis and limousines are required to be licensed under paragraph 31(d) of the License Act [section 47 2331(d)] of the D.C. code at a cost of $25 per year.[17]

As of 1979, there are about 8,400 taxi vehicles that operate in the District of Columbia. Approximately 90 percent of the taxis are owner-operated. The largest fleet operator in the city is the Yellow Cab Company. The Yellow Cab Company owns a fleet of 40 vehicles. In addition, the Company franchises its name to about 900 independent owner-operators. The Yellow Cab Company regulates only those taxis that it owns as a fleet operator.

Consumer groups and individual taxi owner-operators have always taken a stand against placing numerical limits on the number of taxis in the District of Columbia. A typical statement expressing the attitude of owner-operators in D.C. is the following:

> Considering the monopolistic trend that all similar [referring to numerical limitations] practices have taken in other cities where they have been put into operation, it seems as though we could, here in Washington, profit by the mistakes of those who have preceded us in this taxi-control problem. This is the Capitol of the United States and the seat of the Federal Government and as such it is advisable that we shun any legislation that is monopolistic in nature for it is the duty of the Federal Government to oppose monopolies, not to foster them.[18]

Similar sentiments were expressed by the Taxicab Industry Group, which is a loosely knit owner-operator association which represents 43 of the 62 taxi companies and associations and 85 percent of the drivers operating in Washington, D.C.:

> The taxi business is unique here in that approximately 90 percent of the cabs are owner-operated. Therefore, passengers get a better and safer ride because of the driver's personal

interest in his own taxicab. This is not true in other large cities where meters are required and the operation of the taxi system is controlled by fleets. Because he is an independent businessman, as we have previously stated many times, the owner-operator has better equipment and exercises greater care than a driver who is not an owner. It is the independent cab drivers in Washington, D.C., who have given the city the best taxi service of any city in the United States. This is a recognized fact, testified to by the many visitors who ride our cabs as well as many Senators and Congressmen who travel worldwide and know first hand about good service.[19]

A considerable portion of taxi owners have always taken a strong stand against the monopolization of the taxi industry in Washington. Such an attitude is not so much an expression of an ideological persuasion as the fear that monopolization would benefit and foster large fleet operators at the expense of the independent owner-operator.[20]

With open entry the Washington taxi industry consists of mostly self-employed people who work and conduct their business as they see fit. It is estimated that at least 50 percent of the taxi owners are part-time operators who work after and before hours of their regular nontaxi employment. In addition, a number of taxi owners lease their taxis to other individuals on either a full- or part-time basis.

The free market that exists in Washington produces benefits for a large group of people. First it produces business ownership or work opportunities for many semiskilled workers, college students and others wishing to supplement their regular earnings. It provides higher-quality services to consumers at lower prices. It also refutes the disorderly market, "dog-eat-dog" and congestion type of arguments used as justification for strict regulation in other cities.

Table 9 gives information on the taxi industry in the District of Columbia. The Public Service Commission maintains a file on persons licensed to operate a taxi. On each file, there is a picture of the licensee. Therefore, the race of the licensee can be reliably identified. In another file, there is a listing of the membership of the various taxi associations in the District. From this file it can be established

Table 9

Racial/Sexual Composition of Taxi Industry in Washington, D.C., 1979

	OWNED	RENTAL	NEW[a]	NONE[b]	TOTALS
Black Males	1563	479	513	1209	3764
White Males	695	520	235	350	1800
Black Females	66	42	39	108	255
White Females	8	2	13	6	29
Total	2332	1043	800	1673	5848

[a] New licensee, status not yet available

[b] The licensee neither owns nor rents a cab. He has a license on file but according to records is not currently operating a taxicab

whether the licensee owns or rents his taxi. With these two files, race and ownership could be established. The associations selected for use in identifying ownership were Yellow Cab (1365), Capitol Cab (1111), Liberty Cab (410), and Diamond Cab (434). Together these associations accounted for 46 percent of the licensed taxis in Washington.

From one set of files containing nearly 12,000 license holders, we were able to identify the ownership/rental status of 5,848 people by using the membership listing from the above taxi associations. We found that 2,332 such persons owned their taxis. Of this number, there were 1,563 black male owners and 66 black female owners. There were 695 white male owners and 8 white female owners. Therefore, of all owners that we were able to identify, 70 percent of taxis were owned by blacks individually and 30 percent of taxi ownership was held by whites. It is a good possibility that this number is a fair representation of racial ownership for the industry as a whole because officials assisting us with the data estimate that 75 percent of taxi ownership in the District is black ownership.[21]

While a more rigorous investigation would seek a complete record of the licensee file (which consists of more than 20,000 cards, many of which are duplicates for individual license holders), preliminary findings of the Washington

Table 10

Taxis in Major U.S. Cities

City	YEAR OF RESTRICTION	POPULATION IN YEAR OF RESTRICTION*	NUMBER OF TAXIS	TAXIS/ 1,000	1960 POPULATION	NUMBER OF TAXIS IN 1960	TAXIS/ 1,000 1960	1970 POPULATION	NUMBER OF TAXIS 1970	TAXIS/ 1,000 1970	1976 POPULATION	NUMBER OF TAXIS 1976	TAXIS/ 1,000 1976
Washington, D.C.	1930	486,869	4,000	8.2	763,956	10,180	13.3	757,000	9,144	12.1	700,000	9,144	12.0
New Orleans	1972	546,116	1,604	2.9	627,525	1,537	2.54	593,000	1,600	2.7	581,000	1,162	2.0
Boston	1931	781,188	1,525	1.9	697,197	1,525	2.2	641,000	1,525	2.4	618,000	1,525	2.5
New York	1937	297,630	13,556	1.9	781,984	11,782	1.5	895,000	11,722	1.5	7,423,000	11,787	1.6
Chicago	1963	482,140	4,600	1.3	550,404	4,600	1.3	367,000	4,600	1.4	3,074,000	4,600	1.5
Baltimore	1936	804,874	1,151	1.43	939,024	1,151	1.2	906,000	1,525	1.7	827,000	1,078	1.3
San Francisco	NA	759,001	1,310	0.74	742,855	713	0.96	716,000	798	1.1	663,000	711	1.1
Detroit	1946	292,352	NA		670,144	1,310	0.8	511,000	1,310	0.9	1,314,000	1,310	1.0
Houston	1934				938,219	496	0.5	233,000	689	0.6	1,455,000	993	0.7
Indianapolis					476,258	475	0.9	734,000			709,000		
Atlanta					487,455	401	0.82						
Memphis					497,524			624,000	347	.55			
Dallas	1937	260,475	NA		679,684	520	0.8	844,000	520	0.6	668,000	425	0.6
Milwaukee	1924	457,147	170	0.4	741,324	450	0.6	717,000	412	0.6	849,000	517	0.6
San Diego					573,224	304		697,000			661,000	389	0.6
Los Angeles					479,015	885	0.4	816,000	885	0.3	789,000	421	0.5
Phoenix	1928	NA			439,170	99	0.2	582,000	99	0.2	2,244,000	1,100	0.4
Honolulu					291,179	822	2.8				680,000	240	0.3
Cleveland					876,050	586	0.66	751,000			626,000	220	0.3
Philadelphia	1920	823,779	NA		002,512	1,480	0.7	949,000	1,480	0.8	1,797,000	604	0.3

* Population figures based on U.S. Census of Population.

taxi industry are remarkable in comparison to some other U.S. cities that have large black populations—Philadelphia, for example, which has about 14 black taxi owners according to an estimate of the State Commissioner of the Public Utility Commission, Wilson Goode.

Table 10 gives a partial description of the taxicab industry in twenty U.S. cities. As indicated, Washington, D.C., has the largest number of taxis per one thousand of the population. This means that Washington taxi-riders not only receive higher-quality service but they receive that service at prices that are among the lowest in the nation.

In examining the available data, there appears to be little doubt that it is an open taxicab market that benefits would-be taxicab drivers, as it has in Washington, D.C.[22] The only basic difference between the operation of the D.C. taxicab industry and that in nearly every other major city in the U.S. is the nominal license fee and the absence of numerical restrictions on the number of taxis. The Washington case supports the contention made earlier that racial discrimination alone is overused to explain the restricted earning opportunities for blacks.

Restrictive licensing in the taxicab business not only denies opportunity, but it imposes a considerable burden on poor minority communities in another way. This is in the form of reduced transportation for poor communities. Several studies have shown that a considerable part of the taxicab ridership consists of poor people:

> . . . in Boston, households with annual incomes under $4,000 used cabs about as often as those with incomes greater than $10,000; and . . . in New York's Central Brooklyn Model Cities area, one in which 40 percent of the households had annual incomes of $4,000 or less, these latter households accounted for 43 percent of the cab trips generated by that area; 72 percent of the area's cab riders came from households without autos.[23]

Conclusion

A free market in the taxicab industry will not produce a panacea for the disadvantaged. However, it is one small way to upward mobility for some, which has been cut off by government. As such, it demonstrates again one of the key differences between disadvantaged blacks and disadvantaged ethnic groups of the past. A poor illiterate Italian, for example, arriving in our cities in 1925 or 1930 could, if he had ambition and industry, go out and buy a car and write TAXI on it. Thus he could provide upward mobility for his family. Today a poor person of *any* race would find that industry and ambition are not enough, if he sought the same path to upward mobility. He would find the path barricaded by a license costing $20, $30, or $60 thousand—a considerable barrier.

APPENDIX

D.C. Rules and Regulations,
Title 14, Public Service Commission

Procedure For Obtaining A License For
A Passenger Vehicle For Hire Having A Seating
Capacity Of Less Than Eight Passengers

(Sept. 24, 1964)

Taxicabs and limousines (except those used exclusively for funerals) are required to be licensed under Par. 31(d) of the License Act (Sec. 47–2331(d), D.C. Code) at a cost of $25.00 a year. The license year begins on April 1st.

Forms for applying for the license (copy attached hereto) can be obtained from taxicab company or association offices or from the Taxicab Bureau of the Public Service (formerly Public Utilities) Commission of the District of Columbia.

When all information required is furnished on the form, it should be presented with the taxicab to one of the Department of Motor Vehicle inspection stations (see Appendix E for standards) for inspection.

After the vehicle has passed inspection and the Inspection Station stamp has been placed on the license application form, present the form, together with properly executed Certificate of Insurance (Appendix C,

Chapter IV, Title 14, DCRR) from the insurance carrier, to the Taxicab Bureau of the Public Service Commission.

If all information required on the form is correct, the vehicle has been approved by the Inspection Station and the Certificate of Insurance in order, the Taxicab Bureau will put the Public Service Commission's stamp of approval on the license application form. It can then be taken to the Department of Motor Vehicles, Office of Public Vehicle Services, 469 C Street, N.W., (C.O. 69–670, 12–24–69) where, upon the payment of $25.00 for a full year (pro rated for less than a full year), the license will be issued.

Lost License

In the event a license is lost or destroyed, a duplicate can be obtained by submitting an affidavit on the form attached hereto, to the Taxicab Bureau of the Public Service Commission. There is usually a notary public available in the Taxicab Bureau before whom the affidavit can be executed.

Thereafter, the affidavit can be taken to the Office of Public Vehicle Services at the address shown above, where, upon the payment of a $2.00 fee, a duplicate can be issued.

CHAPTER 7

Occupational Licensing of Plumbers and Electricians

There is no worse torture than the torture of laws.

—Francis Bacon
Of Judicature

The law is but words and paper without the hands and swords of men.

—James Harrington
The Commonwealth of Oceana

Brief History

Plumbers were among the first trades to become licensed in the United States. They were first licensed in California in 1885. Most licensing statutes classify plumbers into three groups: master plumbers, journeyman plumbers and apprentice plumbers. Master plumbers can be thought of as employers who are independent businessmen or who act as plumbing contractors.[1] Journeyman plumbers are workers who have been certified as competent and can do the ordinary work of plumbing. Apprentices are untrained men learning the trade either through on-the-job training or formal schooling. State or local plumber-licensing boards are granted the authority to determine all conditions of entry and have police powers to enforce concurrence.

When plumbers were first licensed, the broad issue of constitutionality of such licensing arose in several court cases. Indeed, some early courts struck down state licensing of plumbers as a violation of the Fourteenth Amendment of the United States Constitution. For example, in a Washington case, *State* ex rel. *Richey* v. *Smith,*[2] the court said, in granting a *habeas corpus* to free a plumber who was arrested for working without a license, that the legislature was limited in making laws in the name of public health and safety. The Washington court cited Justice Peckham's opinion in an earlier case:

> Taking the act as a whole . . . its purpose is to enable the employing plumbers to create a sort of guild or body among themselves, into which none is to be permitted to enter excepting as he may pass an examination, the requisites of which are not stated, and where his success or failure is to be determined by a board of which some of their own number are members. . . . It is difficult for me to see the least resemblance to a health regulation in all this.
>
> I think the act is vicious in its purpose and that tends directly to the creation and fostering of a monopoly.[3]

In later years, the courts upheld licensing, including that of plumbers and electricians, as a legitimate expression of the police powers of the state.[4] While courts now hold that licensing is consistent with constitutionally valid use of state police powers, such a decree does not change the effects of licensing, including its effects on minority economic opportunity.

Licensing Out Negroes

Occupational licensing can reduce employment opportunities for Negroes by creating artificial or unrealistic standards. It can occur without apparent racial motivation as in the case of cosmetologists discussed earlier. Or occupational licensing can be used as a tool to achieve certain goals such as the elimination of Negroes from a craft. Occupational licensing coupled with white-dominated craft unions has been a particularly effective tool for reducing employment for Negroes. Craft unions such as the plumbers and electricians *explicitly* advocated licensure laws to eliminate Negro competition. Greene and Woodson wrote, "a favorite method of barring (Negroes) from plumbing and electrical work was to install a system of unfair examinations which were conducted by whites."[5]

An example of one union's desire to eliminate Negro plumbers is contained in the following letter advocating licensing:

> Editor Journal: Norfolk, Va.,
> Dear Sir and Brother: February 12, 1905
>   Enclosed you will find a clipping from a Norfolk paper, which I would suggest that you give space in the next issue of the Journal, believing that it will be of interest to the members of U.A., especially of the southern district, as the Negro is a factor in this section, and I believe the enclosed Virginia state plumbing law which will eliminate him and the imposter from following our craft. . . .
>   (*Signed*) C. H. Perry, Sec. L.U. 110[6]

Enclosed with the letter was a legislative bill containing the following commonly stated justification for the licensing of plumbers: "To promote the public health and to regulate the sanitary construction, house draining, and plumbing, and to secure the registration of plumbers in all cities. . . ."[7]

In a northern trade publication was the following:

> . . . All the other work, jobbing, etc, is done by Negroes. . . . Bro. Becker and a few of the boys are going to run over to Greenville and make a thorough investigation and try to have these bosses hire white men. It is a wonder to me that there are not more Negroes working at our business from the way our members in a great many places use them as helpers. . . . *Plumbers, Gas and Steam Fitters Official Journal* (Chicago, January 1905), vol. X.[8]

In the same issue the *Plumbers, Gas and Steam Fitters Official Journal* contained another entry:

> There are about ten Negro skate plumbers working around
> here [Danville, Va.], doing quite a lot of jobbing and repairing,
> but owing to the fact of not having an examination board
> [licensing agency] it is impossible to stop them, hence the
> anxiety of the men here to organize. *Plumbers, Gas and Steam
> Fitters Official Journal,* January 1905[9]

Proposals for licensing as a means of eliminating black
tradesmen were not restricted to the South. In Kansas City,
Negroes were denied entry into a number of trades including
plumbing and electricity.[10] In New Jersey it was reported
that it was impossible for a Negro to become a licensed
plumber or steam fitter.[11] Spero and Harris, in their study,
found that "in a city like Philadelphia, the licensing board
will not grant a Negro a license—in Chicago the Negro
plumbers have failed to gain advances after years of
effort."[12]

Union Growth and Exclusion of Negroes from the Crafts

Negroes have not always been conspicuously absent or un-
derrepresented in the skilled crafts and trades. Considerable
evidence from the past, albeit anecdotal, suggests that years
ago Negroes were the dominant practitioners in some crafts.

Isaac Weld, in his eighteenth-century travels around the
United States, observed, "Amongst their slaves are found tay-
lors, shoemakers, carpenters, smiths, turners, wheelwrights,
weavers, tanners, etc."[13]

Novelist James Weldon Johnson wrote, "The Negroes
drove the horse and mule teams, they laid the bricks, they
painted the buildings and fences, they loaded and unloaded
ships. When I was a child, I did not know that there existed
such a thing as a white carpenter or bricklayer or plasterer
or tinner."[14]

According to Charles B. Rousseve: "Throughout the
South 'where the majority of white men were too lazy to
work,' by far the largest proportion of labor, skilled and unskilled, was performed by Negroes, both freeman and the
slave."[15]

John Stephen Durham wrote about union exclusion of Negroes from skilled crafts:

In the city of Washington, for example, at one period, some of the finest buildings were constructed by colored workmen. Their employment in large numbers continued some time after the war. The British Legation, the Centre Market, the Freeman's Bank, and at least four well-built schoolhouses are monuments to the acceptability of their work under foremen of their own color. Today, apart from hod-carriers, not a colored workman is to be seen on new buildings, and a handful of jobbers and patchers, with possibly two carpenters who can undertake a large job, are all who remain of the body of colored carpenters and builders and stone-cutters who were generally employed a quarter of a century ago.[16]

Commenting about stevedores, Durham says, "The effective organization of white laborers was closely followed by the driving of Negroes from the levees at the muzzles of loaded rifles. The iron industry is passing through the same experience. . . ."[17] Durham goes on to point out in conclusion, ". . . the real struggle of the unions is in opposition to the general desire of the employing class of the South to give the Negro whatever work he is capable of doing."[18]

Herbert Hill in a summary of Durham's findings writes:

Extending his inquiry into the North, Durham found the effects of the Negro exclusion policy to be even "more manifest." In Philadelphia in 1838, the Society of Friends had compiled a directory of occupations in which Negroes were employed. Significantly included were such skilled jobs as cabinet maker, plumber, printer, sailmaker, ship's carpenter, stone cutter and many others. By the end of the 1890's, Negroes had been forced out of most of these and other craft occupations.[19]

Herbert Hill continues his documentation of the impact of unions on Negro craft employment opportunities:

In the older seaboard cities of the South, Negroes had once been employed in a great variety of occupations, skilled and unskilled. However, in the last decades of the nineteenth century the process of Negro displacement had begun, and trade unions were a most important part of this development. . . . in both South and North the trade union opposes black labor wherever it can and admits it to fellowship only as a last resort.[20]

It does not take too much search to conclude that the absence of Negroes from the crafts, including electricians and plumbers, is a result of a tradition of racial exclusion policies by labor unions. The International Brotherhood of Electrical Workers and the United Association of Plumbers and Steamfitters unions have traditionally excluded Negroes from membership by tacit agreement among their members.[21]

There is no question about union exclusionary policy and practices of the past. But what can be said about today? More than likely there is little evidence of flagrant racial exclusion. But somehow in many craft unions black membership is virtually absent. Such an outcome can be explained in several ways that are perhaps interrelated. One is that people may not seek entry to the union because they view their chances as being slim because there are relatively few black journeymen electricians or plumbers. Second, entry conditions are artificially raised so as to discourage entry. This is related to a third possible reason: the whole package of entry conditions that include long apprenticeship periods and restrictions on the number of apprentices, seniority rules, and artificially high wages and licensure—all these tend to discriminate against lower skilled tradesmen.

Negro Opportunity in Electrical and Plumbing Work Today

Racial discrimination by occupational licensing boards is not just a historical curiosity made irrelevant by racial enlightenment of today. Benjamin Shimberg reports:

The only licensed Negro plumber in Montgomery County, Alabama at the time of this study reported that he had spent four years learning the plumbing trade at Talladega College, but that when he attempted to obtain a license, he faced seemingly insurmountable barriers. He took the local examination and was told each time that he failed. He was not told what his score was nor was he allowed to see his examination paper. Finally he took and passed the state master plumber's examination and then managed to use his state license as a means of obtaining a local license in Montgomery County.[22]

Shimberg reports that black electricians face similar difficulty in Alabama. Union-sponsored electrical apprenticeship programs appear closed to them. The union requirement is that all applicants must be high school graduates. High school equivalency test certificates are not accepted. Final selection to the apprenticeship training programs is determined on the basis of a personal interview, which gives considerable latitude for racial discrimination.[23]

Professor Shimberg insightfully concludes his analysis of the problems that blacks have in entering licensed crafts such as plumbing and electrical work by pointing out that the vested economic interests that are protected from competition by state licensing boards cannot be persuaded to change their practices voluntarily and: ". . . nor is there much room for optimism that many state legislatures or city councils would be willing to incur the wrath of powerful labor unions or affluent trade associations whose members derive economic benefits from the perpetuation of the status quo."[24]

Even though we now live in what is called an age of racial enlightenment, there is evidence that licensing and unionization consistently work to the disadvantage of blacks. Some evidence comes in the form of black membership in the major electrical and plumbing unions in the building trades. According to Equal Employment Opportunity Commission (EEOC) data, in 1969, Negroes constituted 1.9 percent of the membership of the International Brotherhood of Electrical Workers (IBEW) and they constituted 0.6 percent of the International Plumbers and Pipefitters.[25] By 1972 their membership had risen to 6.5 and 4.4 percent respectively.[26] In a study of the "mechanical" trades (boilermakers, electrical workers, elevator constructors, iron workers, plumbers and pipefitters, and sheetmetal workers), Herbert Hammerman found that in 1972, 58 percent of the local unions had no Negro or Spanish-origin members.[27]

While the number of Negro union members is not a perfect measure of racial discrimination, it does suggest that licensing and unionization may have an ongoing adverse impact on minority chances to become plumbers and electricians. The issue of occupational entry barriers, whether they are those imposed by state licensing authorities or by labor organizations, is not whether open racial discrimination is practiced. The issue is, so far as policy is concerned, what is the racial effect of artificial barriers to entry?

There is evidence that occupational licensing is used in other ways that handicap minorities. This happens when incumbent practitioners attempt to protect their jobs in the face of a slack market for their services. Professor Alex Maurizi investigated the relationships between a slack market for labor in licensed occupations and the examination pass rate.[28] He found that a substantial, and statistically significant, portion of the pass rate was explained by the excess demand. In other words, when there was unemployment in the licensed trade, the difficulty level of the examination rose in order to reduce the number of new entrants. Obviously, such a technique to protect the incomes of incumbent practitioners is going to have its greatest discriminatory impact on the groups in the population who have less and poorer education. Minorities are disproportionately represented in such a population.

The discussion would be incomplete if it were not mentioned that blacks are not the only group targeted for discriminatory licensing. During the 1930s virtually every occupational licensure law was amended. They were amended to add U.S. citizenship as a new requirement. One might ask what public health safety interest is served by stipulating that a tradesman, otherwise qualified, be a U.S. citizen? There is none. However, during the 1930s there was a large migration of Jews to the United States as a result of the hostilities in Europe. Many of these immigrants, which included non-Jews as well, were skilled artisans. The U.S. citizenship requirement was an effective way to forestall their entry into licensed occupations which served the interests of incumbent licensees.[29]

Some Other Adverse Effects of Licensing

Restricted entry, through licensing, places disadvantaged people at a severe handicap without necessarily improving the quality of services received by the consumer, the often stated (pretended) beneficiary of the regulation. In fact, one study showed that there is a significant relationship between occupational licensing and the number of accidental deaths by electrocution. The more stringent the state licensing examination, the fewer the electricians, hence the higher are the prices of an electrician's services; therefore, the greater the willingness of amateurs to undertake electrical wiring tasks and risk electrocution in the process.[30] Aside from this adverse impact of licensing, it produces what the authors, Carroll and Gaston, call the "Cadillac effect." By having high requirements for entry, licensing provides high-quality services for *high-income* people. But those people who have low incomes, who cannot afford to pay the higher prices, are forced either to do without the service, to do the work themselves, or to rely upon low-priced unlicensed quacks or charlatans. As far as electrical services are concerned, strict licensing requirements may account for a significant portion of fires of electrical origin. That is because of high electrician fees caused by restrictive licensing. Owing to high prices some people make their own electrical repairs ineptly or fail to make them at all.

What Can Be Done?

Presently there are few legal remedies that promise to be effective in eliminating the anticompetitive features of occupational licensure. Federal antitrust laws offer little hope because of the *Parker* doctrine. The *Parker* doctrine emerged from a 1943 U.S. Supreme Court decision that held that antitrust statutes apply to *private* acts of collusion which restrain competition.[31] The Court held that collusion in the restraint of competition was sanctioned if it was done by the state. The reason that the Court took its position was that it thought that wide application of antitrust laws to state regulatory practices would create a crisis in federalism.

One possible remedy for restrictive licensing can be found in another U.S. Supreme Court case, *Griggs* v. *Duke*.[32] This decision held that racial discrimination has been reinforced by tests which are actually unrelated to successful job performance, and employers have been ordered to eliminate this kind of testing. Much of the testing for licensure is unrelated to successful job performance. As such, *Griggs* v. *Duke* may be a partial remedy sought by public interest lawyers.

Ultimately, occupational licensing is a political problem. Power interest groups representing various occupations, through lobbying, have used the coercive powers of the state to protect their incomes from competition. Whether the general public can politically defeat narrow interests is a debatable issue. All evidence suggests that the narrow interests are the superior political force.

CHAPTER 8

Negroes and
the Railroad Industry*

One of the most significant things that I saw in the South—
and I saw it everywhere—was the way in which white
people were torn between their feelings of race prejudice
and their downright economic needs.

—Ray Stannard Baker, 1908

THE RAILROAD INDUSTRY has historically been the site of
the most virulent forms of racially discriminatory employment policy by unions. There are several factors that made
this possible. First, union organization in the railroad industry has traditionally been along craft lines. Second, unions
in the railroad industry, having launched collective bargaining as early as the 1880s, are among the oldest and the strongest of American unions. Third, the railroad unions were significantly strengthened by government protection during
World War I and later by the Railway Labor Act, as amended
in 1934, which outlawed yellow-dog contracts and the forma-
tion of company-dominated or company-financed unions.[1]
The effects of these factors are of such importance that some
detail will be useful on how union racial discrimination and
government support combined to reduce and virtually eliminate jobs for Negroes in the railroad industry.

The National Mediation Board (NMB), created by the
1934 amendments to the Railway Act of 1926, was to mediate

---

* Adapted from my article, "Freedom to Contract Blacks and Labor
Organizations" in *Black America and Organized Labor: A Fair Deal*
(Washington, D.C., The Lincoln Institute, 1980), pp. 10–32.

labor disputes arising on railroads. One of the practices of the NMB was that of defining the bargaining unit that was to represent railroad employees. The NMB nearly always defined the unit to suit the jurisdictional claims of the particular railway union under consideration.[2]

Negroes who were not accepted for membership in most locals or were relegated to a low status in the railroad unions during this time naturally attempted to form their own unions. These attempts were nullified by the action of the National Mediation Board, which simply ruled that these alternative unions created by discriminated-against Negroes could not represent black employees who were unfairly being represented by the bargaining unit given exclusive rights by the board. In effect, the board bestowed monopoly representation powers to white labor unions that were discriminatory in refusing equal membership rights to Negroes.

The adverse effects of this policy stand out in stark relief in the case of *Brotherhood of Railway and Steamship Clerks* v. *United Transport Service Employees of America* (UTSEA).[3] The court in this case was asked to settle the conflicting claims of two unions competing for the rights to represent forty-five Negro porters at a train station in St. Paul, Minnesota. The porters were ineligible for membership in the Brotherhood of Railway and Steamship Clerks Union because they were Negro; they unanimously voted for UTSEA as their bargaining agent. The NMB dismissed the application of UTSEA on the ground that the porters were not a separate class of employees and that there was no dispute over representation. The court held that the Brotherhood of Railway and Steamship Clerks represented porters.

The federal district court, upon appeal, declared the dismissal order void. The Court of Appeals pointed out that the dismissal forced the Negro employees to accept representation by an organization in which they had no right to membership or right to speak or be heard on their own behalf. However, the Negro workers' victory was not to be had. The United States Supreme Court reversed the Appeals Court decision on the ground that the Mediation Board's certifications are not subject to judicial review.

During this era and later there were numerous certification proceedings that granted discriminatory labor unions
exclusive bargaining representation.[4]

The racially discriminatory practices of railway labor
unions, reinforced by national labor laws, gave rise to several important court cases. Chief among these cases was
Steele v. *Louisville & Nashville Railroad.*[5] This case involved a Negro fireman, B. W. Steele, who had been laid
off as a result of the Southeastern Carrier's Agreement, an
agreement between several railroad companies and railway
labor organizations. Steele had been working as a fireman
along with three other Negro firemen in the high-paying
passenger division of the Louisville and Nashville line. The
union declared that the jobs of the four Negroes were vacant.
The jobs were later filled by white firemen having less seniority.

When Steele first started working in 1910, 98 percent
of the firemen in his Louisville and Nashville district were
Negro. By 1943 the proportion of Negroes had dropped to
20 percent hired as firemen. Steele's case was originally held
before the Alabama Supreme Court. The court found that,
as a certified representative of the firemen, the brotherhood
had the right to destroy or create rights of members of the
bargaining unit. However, when the United States Supreme
Court heard the case it reversed the decision of the state
court and found that the union had violated the Railway
Labor Act. In reaching its decision, the Court recognized
that the Railway Labor Act would be on very weak constitutional grounds if it denied individuals *both* the right to bargain for themselves and the right to be fairly represented
by the exclusive bargaining unit. The U.S. Supreme Court
ruled that "the Railway Labor Act imposes on the bargaining
representative of a craft or class of employees the duty to
exercise fairly the power conferred upon it in behalf of all
those for whom it acts, without hostile discrimination
against them."[6] Despite the Supreme Court ruling, effective
discrimination against Negro railroad workers did not end:
the mechanism for the maintenance of effective discrimination had not been weakened—namely, the monopoly powers
conferred upon unions by the federal government. The

Brotherhood of Locomotive Firemen ignored the Court decision and maintained the illegal Southeastern Carrier's Agreement. It was not until the 1950s, following separate law suits awarding damages, that the effect of the Steele decision was even modestly felt.[7]

In the late 1940s, unions began to employ subtler techniques that had the effect of reducing or eliminating Negro firemen. For example, the Brotherhood of Locomotive Firemen began a campaign in 1947 that, superficially at least, appeared to be aimed at rejecting its racially discriminatory practices of the past by negotiation of an agreement that struck out the anti-Negro quota clause. However, this was nothing but a strategy to win gains that had been lost through litigation throughout the forties. The new contract contained a clause stipulating that only those firemen who were "promotable" were to be employed on freight and passenger train runs. All others could be employed only in yards.

In January 1948 the Brotherhood of Locomotive Firemen proposed to the members of the Southeastern Carrier's Conference a test to determine whether a fireman was promotable. Failing the test after three tries would mean that the man was unpromotable and would be dismissed from the service. Obviously, the test was directed at eliminating Negro firemen. Most Negro firemen had been hired many years ago and there had been no education requirements. The test based on the hiring requirement for engineers would have caused the Negroes to be dismissed. Fortunately, for the Negro firemen around the country, the courts held that the test was illegal.

One of the most remarkable stories to be told about the early history of Negroes in the railroad industry is their success despite white worker hostility. As such this story demonstrates that racial discrimination, in and of itself, cannot generally explain Negro unemployment. But it may explain lower wages.

The turn of the century in the United States saw considerable hostility against Negroes, particularly in the railroad industry. Some of the hostility involved the murder of Negroes. Trainmen and firemen, while able effectively to bar Negroes from union membership, could not bar them from their craft. In the South, where hostility toward Negro workmen was the greatest, some railroad companies had firemen crews that were 85 to 90 percent Negro. For southern states as a whole, Negroes constituted 27 percent of the brakemen, and 12 percent of the switchmen. These statistics changed dramatically in later years. By 1940, 18 percent of the firemen in the South were Negroes, falling to 7 percent by 1960.[8] W. E. B. Dubois, writing of this period, concluded, "The great railway systems too discriminate against the Negro, and here his opportunity is limited, no matter how high a degree of efficiency he may attain, to the menial and poorly paid tasks."[9] Frequently, according to Dubois, unionization meant the redesignation of "Negro jobs" as "white man's work," forcing Negroes out of jobs they traditionally held.

This changing employment picture in the railroad industry is of considerable interest and supportive of the general hypothesis suggested in this essay. Table 11 gives the number of black and white firemen by years and regions. It shows the fall in the number of firemen in general since 1920. But most remarkable is the decline of black firemen compared to white firemen after 1920. The decline of black firemen was the greatest in the South, where, at one time, they were the most numerous by percentage.

The high rate of employment for Negroes in the railroad industry was not at all a result of benevolence on behalf of white owners and managers of railroads. It existed because Negroes would work for wages that were often just two-thirds of the wages paid to white firemen for doing the same job. The wage differential had the clear effect of reducing the power of white firemen to demand higher wages. As one white fireman put it, "Everytime the firemen ask for an increase in wages or for overtime due them, they are told by the superintendent, 'Why, I can get a Negro in your place for one dollar, while I'm paying you $1.50 per day.' "[10]

Railroad companies were very much interested in keeping the Negro in their employ because hiring Negroes meant

Table 11
Locomotive Firemen in the U.S. by Region, 1910–60 (Males Only)

REGION		1910 WHITE	1910 BLACK*	1920 WHITE	1920 BLACK**	1930 WHITE	1930 BLACK	1940 WHITE	1940 BLACK	1950 WHITE	1950 BLACK	1960 WHITE	1960 BLACK
SOUTH	Abs. #	14,755	5,012	17,722	5,878	14,309	4,254	9,545	2,114	12,690	1,823	9,563	750
	Percent	(74.6)	(25.4)	(75.1)	(24.9)	(77.1)	(22.9)	(81.9)	(18.1)	(87.4)	(12.6)	(92.7)	(7.3)
	Abs. Change	—	—	2,967	866	−3,413	−1,624	−4,764	−2,140	3,145	−291	−3,127	−1,073
	% Change	—	—	20.1	17.3	−19.3	−27.6	−33.3	−50.3	32.9	−13.8	−24.6	−58.9
NORTH CENTRAL	Abs. #	28,353	105	32,762	359	23,814	234	15,430	88	20,063	250	13,925	62
	Percent	(99.6)	(.4)	(98.9)	(1.1)	(99.0)	(1.0)	(99.4)	(.6)	(98.8)	(1.2)	(99.6)	(.4)
	Abs. Change	—	—	4,409	254	−8,948	−125	−8,384	−146	4,633	162	−6,138	−188
	% Change	—	—	15.5	241.9	−27.3	−34.8	−35.2	−62.4	30.0	184.1	−30.6	−75.2

NORTH EAST												
Abs. #	19,202	53	24,765	217	17,128	138	11,341	54	12,080	123	7,545	33
Percent	(99.7)	(.3)	(99.1)	(.9)	(99.2)	(.8)	(99.5)	(.5)	(99.0)	(1.0)	(99.6)	(.4)
Abs. Change	—	—	5,563	164	−7,637	−79	−5,787	−84	739	69	−4,535	−90
% Change	—	—	29.0	309.4	−30.8	−36.4	−33.8	−60.9	6.5	127.8	−37.5	−73.2
WEST												
Abs. #	8,883	18	9,611	31	6,122	14	5,258	7	6,872	26	5,071	5
Percent	(99.8)	(.2)	(99.7)	(.3)	(99.8)	(.2)	(99.9)	(.1)	(99.6)	(.4)	(99.9)	(.1)
Abs. Change	—	—	728	13	−3,489	−17	−864	−7	1,614	19	−1,801	−21
% Change	—	—	8.2	72.2	−36.3	−54.8	−14.1	−50.0	30.7	271.4	−26.2	−80.8

SOURCES: U.S. Department of Commerce, Bureau of the Census, *Census of the Population: 1910*, vol. 2, *Occupations*, Table 2 (Washington, D.C.: Government Printing Office, 1910).

——, *Census of the Population: 1920*, vol. 4, *Occupations*, Table 15, p. 66.

——, *Census of the Population: 1930*, vol. 4, *Occupations by State*, Table 11.

——, *Census of the Population: 1940*, vol. 3, *The Labor Force*, Table 63, p. 91.

——, *Census of the Population: 1950*, vol. 2, pt. 1, *Detailed Characteristics*, Table 139, pp. 1-397.

——, *Census of the Population: 1960*, vol. 1, pt. 1D, *Detailed Characteristics*, Table 257, p. 717.

* U.S. Department of Commerce, Bureau of the Census, *Negro Population: 1790-1915*, *Occupation*, Table 17, pp. 517-520.

** U.S. Department of Commerce, Bureau of the Census, *Census of the Population: 1920*, vol. 4, *Occupations*, Ch. 7, Table 1, pp. 874-1048.

a lower cost of operation. White firemen naturally protested, using allegations of Negro incompetency, large-scale crippling strikes, intimidation and murder.

In 1909 a bitter strike action was taken against the Georgia Railroad. The Brotherhood of Locomotive Firemen demanded that Negroes be completely eliminated from the road. Instead of recommending the elimination of Negroes as was demanded by the union, the arbitration board decided that Negro firemen, hostlers and hostlers' helpers must be paid wages that were *equal* to the wages of white men doing the same job.[11] The Brotherhood of Locomotive Firemen expressed delight with this decision. They said, "If this course is followed by the company and the incentive for employing Negroes thus removed, the strike will not have been in vain."[12]

Why would the Brotherhood of Locomotive Firemen be happy with the decision for equal-pay-for-equal-work? The reason is that if railroads were required to pay blacks the same as they paid whites, the cost to the railroad of discriminating against blacks in employment would in effect be zero. The work pay rule would effectively prevent blacks from competing with whites: the white firemen knew this and knew it well. They knew that they could trust economic incentives to further their racist objectives better than custom, gentlemen's agreements or feelings of white brotherhood.

The understanding of the power of economic inducement to further the cause of racial discrimination in employment is further seen in an agreement between the Brotherhood of Railway Trainmen and the Southern Railroad Association signed in Washington, D.C., in January 1910:

No larger percentage of Negro firemen or yardmen will be employed in any division or in any yard than was employed on January 1, 1910. If on any roads this percentage is now larger than on January 1, 1910, this agreement does not contemplate the discharge of any Negroes to be replaced by whites; but as vacancies are filled or new men employed, whites are to be taken until the percentage of January first is again reached.

Negroes are not to be employed as baggagemen, flagmen or yard foremen, but in any case in which they are so now employed, they are not to be discharged to make places for whites, but when the positions they occupy become vacant, whites shall be employed in their places.

Where no difference in the rates of pay between white and colored exists, the restrictions as to percentage of Negroes to be employed does not apply.[13]

This famous Washington Agreement shows the understanding of and confidence in the power of economic inducement for racial discrimination. As seen by the above citation, while the white firemen insisted on hard and fast quotas for the hiring of Negroes, they recognized that these discriminatory measures were not necessary where the wages between the races were equal. In fact, they perhaps realized that if they insisted on racial quotas where wages were equal, that might result in reduced employment opportunities for white firemen.

Firemen brotherhoods, fresh from their victory with southeast railroads, followed up by negotiating a similar agreement on the railroads in the Mississippi Valley. These agreements, with the full backing of government and monopolistic labor laws, led to the virtual elimination of Negroes from all but the most menial jobs on railroads. Railroad companies were coerced and blackmailed not to hire Negroes as a condition for labor peace.

Charles Houston, who was the lawyer for many black railwaymen, points out how the government failed in its job. Government officials permitted white unions to assist in writing the 1934 Railway Act. Furthermore, each brotherhood had its representative sitting on the First Division of the National Railway Adjustment Board, which had jurisdiction over all grievances affecting train and engine service employment.[14]

Racist Union Policy Toward Others: A Digression

Samuel Gompers, the first president of the American Federation of Labor (AF of L), is mistakenly revered by many as the benevolent father of the labor movement. He is looked at as not having a single racist bone in his body. The evidence shows that Gompers not only led the racist labor movement against blacks but he led it against Orientals as well.

In 1906 the AF of L called for immigration restrictions. The AF of L according to Gompers believed that "the maintenance of the nation depended upon the maintenance of racial purity and strength."[15] The most comprehensive statement of Gompers's feelings about Orientals is found in a pamphlet that he coauthored with Herman Gutstat, an AF of L official. The pamphlet is entitled *Some Reasons for Chinese Exclusion: Meat vs Rice, American Manhood Against Coolieism—Which Shall Survive.*[16] According to Gompers the Chinese were congenitally immoral: "The Yellow man found it natural to lie, cheat and murder and ninety-nine out of one hundred Chinese are gamblers." Gompers did say that Chinese were good workers in American households, but "he goes [the Chinese] joyfully back to his slum and his burrow to the grateful luxury of his normal surroundings—vice, filth, and an atmosphere of horror."[17]

In other speeches, letters and writings, Gompers and other high officials made it clear that similar feelings, and subsequent union practice, extended to Japanese, Koreans and Mexican-Americans.[18]

CHAPTER 9

Interstate Commerce Commission Truck Regulation

Experience should teach us to be most on our guard to protect liberty when the Government's purposes are beneficent. Men born to freedom are naturally alert to repel invasion of their liberty by evil minded rulers. The greatest dangers to liberty lurk in the insidious encroachment by men of zeal, well meaning but without understanding.

—Louis Brandeis

EVERYONE WHO *can* own a truck and *can* drive a truck is not allowed by law to do so. Trucking is regulated. National regulation of the transportation industry originated in 1887 with the Act to Regulate Commerce. This act established the Interstate Commerce Commission. The act originally applied only to the railroad industry. The purpose of the act was to "stabilize" the railroad industry, which was fraught with practices such as rebates, price discrimination and secret rate-cutting.

For a long time, railroad companies tried to form collusive agreements among themselves. But the collusive agreements would always break down because unfaithful partners would cheat on price. The price cheating (cutting price) would take customers away from the faithful collusion members. Therefore, the faithful would have no other choice but to start cutting prices themselves. Thus price wars would develop which would be painful to all the railroad companies.

The railroad companies had considerable interest in seeking government control and regulation. This meant that when the railroad companies got together and colluded on price, they would be successful in doing so. The reason is that the cheating partner to the collusion would be punished by government. The punishment for charging a lower price would be heavy fines, imprisonment or the loss of the right to do business.

Control over the railroads was also sought by some shippers who used the railroad services. Shippers were concerned about the competitive disadvantage they would face if some shippers were granted rebates or low prices by railroads and others were not. The shipper who received the rebate, or lower price, would have cost advantage over his competitor who did not. The favored shipper would be able to entice customers away from the unfavored shipper through charging lower prices or he would be able to attract more investors through higher profits.

The early history of the Interstate Commerce Commission was essentially that of controlling entry and setting minimum and maximum rates and conditions for new construction within the railroad industry.[1] The Motor Carrier Act of 1935 extended the authority of the Interstate Commerce Commission to the regulation of the trucking and bus industries. The chief source of political pressure for the regulation of the trucking industry came from the Interstate Commerce Commission and the railroad industry. At the time of the Motor Carrier Act, most legislative debate on trucking associations stood in opposition. The National Industrial Traffic League, National Highway Users Conference, American Trucking Association, the Automobile Manufacturers Association and the National Association of Motor Bus Operators were all against regulation.[2] Railroads supported the Motor Carrier Act of 1935 because trucks began to make significant inroads into a freight business that had become dominated by the railroad industry.

The railroad industry had become a cartel with the support of the Interstate Commerce Act of 1887. The police power of the Interstate Commerce Commission was used to enforce price agreements and other practices among railroad companies. But with the advent of the truck and its widespread application, the railroad industry lost much of its monopoly power. Truck companies not only matched the rail rates (sometimes they offered lower rates) but they were able to provide what many shippers considered superior services, namely, door-to-door service. Former chief of the Civil Aeronautics Board, Alfred Kahn, said, ". . . the Motor Carrier Act was passed and has been enforced with the explicit purpose and effect of protecting railroads against the intensified competition of motor carriers and protecting motor carriers from one another."[3]

Opportunities in Trucking for Minorities

Interstate motor carrier business is an activity that would offer a person with little money and little education a business ownership opportunity were it not for various forms of government regulations. The initial outlay required to own a tractor for the purposes of hauling, say, household goods, is quite modest. To purchase a late model used tractor costs $15,000. With a standard down-payment of 20 to 25 percent, the buyer needs an initial outlay of $3,000 to $4,000 for a suitable tractor (the selling price of a new tractor is $40,000 and $8,000 to $10,000 down is standard in the trade).[4] Other expenses such as insurance, vehicle registration, inspection and a radio make the initial outlay costs to enter the trucking business (assuming a used tractor) approximately $8,000.

With the relatively low entry costs in terms of skills and initial money outlay, there is still no guarantee that a person can become a truck owner-operator. For many a prospective entrant there are insurmountable entry barriers created by the Interstate Commerce Commission.

Barriers to Entry

Not everyone who wishes to own and operate a truck for the purposes of transporting goods across state lines is permitted to do so. People who are permitted receive a certificate of authority (or authorization) from the ICC. These certificates are transferable to persons other than those originally granted the authority.

Today there are approximately 16,000 certificates, which have been obtained in one of two ways. One way is to purchase it from someone to whom it has already been issued. The purchase price has been estimated to be 15 to 20 percent of the certificate holder's gross sales.[5-6] The second way to get a certificate of authority is to make an application to the Interstate Commerce Commission. The applicant must meet the conditions of the Interstate Commerce Act. Its basic requirement is:

> Whether the new operation or service will serve a useful public purpose, responsive to public demand or need; whether this purpose can and will be served as well by existing lines or carriers; and whether it can be served by the applicant with the new operation or service proposed *without endangering or impairing the operations of existing carriers contrary to the public interest.*[7]

A major part of this requirement, in addition to proving public need and necessity, is that the applicant must show that by his entry he will not take business away from trucking companies already supplying services along the route the applicant proposes to serve. When there is an Interstate Commerce Commission applicant hearing, existing truckers have the right to attend the hearings. They nearly always exercise this right, and nearly always protest the granting of new authorization. Numerous studies have shown that the primary effect of the Motor Carrier Act has been to protect the incumbent trucking companies against new competition.[8]

The application process itself serves as an effective barrier to entry. The applicant must retain legal services specialized in the administrative law of the Interstate Commerce Act. He must have shippers to support his application, *and* the application process can go on for years and have no guarantee of being successful. In one recent case, a black trucking company spent over $300,000 in legal fees and other costs seeking authority to haul household goods across all the states.[9]

This case is particularly interesting because it highlights the difficulties faced by anyone seeking national shipping authority from the Interstate Commerce Commission. Allstates Moving Company has been in operation since 1929. It has twenty-five employees and annual sales of $200,000. The owner has sought to acquire broad national authority, which would allow it to operate in every state. The company started its appeal to the Interstate Commerce Commission in the late 1950s. At the ICC hearings on his petition, the owner has borne the formidable burden of attempting to prove that his services are "needed." In opposition to Allstates' bid for national moving authority are the major moving companies whose annual revenues are well in excess of $100 million.

Allstates is somewhat unique in its efforts because national operating permits are seldom sought, because the ICC seldom grants them. They are expensive if one wants to buy them from an existing holder. Thomas G. Moore, of Stanford University, estimates that a permit, such as that requested by the Allstates Moving Company, if purchased from an existing major moving company would sell for over $15 million.

Minority Participation in Motor Carrier Transportation

The overall impact of ICC restrictive regulations can be more readily seen by looking at minority participation in the trucking industry. According to the American Trucking Association (ATA), "The vast majority of operating rights existing today arose under what is referred to as the 'grandfather' clause in the Act."[10] In other words, when the motor truck industry was brought under the control of the ICC in 1935, approximately 18,000 existing carriers were given operating authority by the ICC. While the operating rights today are reduced in number, mainly because of mergers, these grandfathered operating rights make up the bulk of the operating rights existing today. Minorities, in any significant numbers, were not present in the trucking business in 1935 when these rights were given away. Because they are newcomers, they are heavily penalized by the system, even though entry costs in terms of physical requirements are quite modest compared to other business activities.

How Many Black Truckers?

Since the race of motor carriers is not a statistic known to the ICC it is difficult to state accurately the number of minority carriers with ICC authorization certificates. However, there have been recent efforts to estimate this number by the ICC with the assistance of the Minority Trucking-Transportation Development Corporation (MTTDC).

According to the ICC 1979 report, there are about 133 minority motor freight carriers with ICC authority.[11] There are a total of 16,874 ICC–authorized motor freight carriers in the U.S. Therefore, approximately 0.8 percent of ICC authorization certificates are held by black truckers. *No* black truckers (except Frank Pierson of Allstates Moving Company) have nationwide authority, which is particularly useful in the household goods industry. The report further estimates that of the 133 minority carriers with ICC authorization, 5 are Class I carriers, 13 are Class II carriers, and 115 are Class III carriers.[12] Furthermore, more than 80 percent of ICC certificates of authority held by minorities have been held for less than twenty years.

According to a survey of minority truckers in 1975 to determine their assistance needs, minority truckers were virtually unanimous in their agreement that obtaining interstate authority was their major obstacle to growth and increased business.[13] Other obstacles cited were difficulties in securing contracts for carrying shipments and in obtaining loans for working capital and equipment acquisition. The latter two obstacles are inherently related to the problem of getting ICC (or state) operating authority. Shippers are reluctant to make contracts with carriers having no authority and banks are reluctant to grant loans for working capital and equipment acquisition when a trucker does not have shipping contracts and authority. Compounding this difficulty is the ICC's reluctance to grant authority when a prospective carrier does not demonstrate and meet the "fitness" requirement of the Interstate Commerce Act.

Government Programs to Assist Minority Truckers

Several government programs under the force of Executive Order 11625, under the general rubric of affirmative action, have been instituted to give minorities a greater share of government shipping business. Some of these programs are outlined in a Government Accounting Office report, "Minority Motor Carriers Can Be Given More Opportunity to Participate in Defense Transportation."[14] The Department of Defense (DOD) issued guidelines aimed at increasing minority participation in DOD business and has been asked to implement these guidelines more effectively by the Government Accounting Office (GAO). Part of the GAO recommendations say: "Set up specific objectives, goals, and methodologies for increasing the use of minority carriers."[15]

A significant part of federal agency affirmative action plans are set up in conjunction with the Small Business Administration (SBA) section 8(a) program. Section 8(a) of the Small Business Administration Act of 1953 permits the SBA to enter into contracts with federal agencies and then subcontract the work out to small businesses that meet the SBA program criteria. Under the section 8(a) program, a government agency can select a high-cost carrier and pay him the competitive price with the SBA making up the difference between that price and the *contracted* price, which is higher.

There are other aspects of affirmative action programs for minorities in trucking which are not of significant interest here. What is of interest, however, are the various inequities involved and various government laws and programs that work at cross-purposes. Interstate Commerce Act regulations are just one of many federal laws that handicap minorities in their efforts to enter the mainstream of American society. The law does not have this as its explicit intent, but the effect of the law is precisely that. Interstate Commerce trucking regulation tends to discriminate against latecomers to the trucking industry, those most unable to bear the costly and time-consuming application process and those with little political clout and are outside the "insider" network. In this sense, the Interstate Commerce Act discriminates against whole classes of American citizens. A disproportionate burden of this discrimination is borne by blacks because they are most likely to be in the group of people bearing the aforementioned characteristics.

When original monopoly privileges, in the form of ICC authorization certificates, were issued, blacks in many places did not possess basic Bill of Rights guarantees, much less trucks. Surely they did not have the business rights that those had who received the 18,000 grandfathered privileges. When the Motor Carrier Act was enacted in 1935, there were a few black-owned companies in the business of interstate trucking. The authorization certificates of most, if not all, of them were revoked. The reason was that in those days insurance companies, by and large, did not write insurance policies for blacks. There is at least one black who was able to keep this authority by having a shipper fraudulently list his race as white on his insurance application.[16]

Many minorities are already in the general transportation business. Nationally, according to the 1972 Survey of Minority-Owned Business Enterprises, there are 12,917 minority-owned transportation companies.[17] The survey category is broad, so this number does not represent only people who own trucks; some offer transportation-related services.[18] Most minority-owned trucking companies are individual owner-operators.

Most minority truckers are in the local sector of the trucking business. Very few are in the more lucrative interstate trucking market. It is estimated that only 133 blacks hold certificates of authority which entitle them to operate independently in the interstate sector of the trucking industry. Contrary to the situation in many other areas of business, the minority problem is not capitalization and business acumen. Their problem was summarized by Timothy Person, citing testimony by Samuel Cornelius, deputy director of the Office of Minority Business Enterprise, to the Subcommittee on Housing, Minority Enterprise and Economic Development of the Congressional Black Caucus:

> . . . the share which minority truckers have of the interstate trucking market is infinitesimally small, apparently less than one-tenth of 1 percent. Why is this the case? Is it a matter of difficulty in capitalization, lack of an experience base in the industry, or disinterest of shippers? After examining this situation we must answer this question with a resounding no.
>
> The extent of capitalization required by firms entering the trucking industry or expanding from local hauling to interstate service is modest compared to the revenue potential of such growth. . . . In addition, there is no lack of minority firms with trucking experience. . . . The incredibly small participation of minority firms in the interstate trucking is without question due in large part to the severely restrictive entry criteria mandated by the Interstate Commerce Act.
>
> The Interstate Commerce Commission must labor under the burdens of this archaic act when determining the award of operating rights. The effect of this act is to place enormous barriers in the way of minority truckers. These barriers are fully as restrictive as the discredited practices of the Jim Crow system that barred entry into public facilities and many professions.[19]

Uniquely neither to minorities nor to the trucking industry, when government actions or policies hurt one group of citizens in order to benefit another group of citizens, there is usually clamor for enactment of a policy that will help the group of citizens originally hurt by the government action. The governmental assistance given this group will typically hurt some other group. Marc Connelly, in the Negro play *Green Pastures,* expressed what may be the dilemma of privilege-granting activities of government in a passage where God says to the angel Gabriel: "Every time Ah passes a miracle, Ah have to pass fo' or five mo' to ketch up wid it."

Ex Parte Number 278, Equal Opportunity in Surface Transportation, is one such policy instituted by the Interstate Commerce Commission in an attempt to offset the government-created disadvantage that confronts minorities in the trucking industry.[20] The purpose of *Ex Parte Number 278* is to increase and assist minority participation in the shipment of government goods. The commission's function under *Ex Parte 278* is to expedite the application procedure for disadvantaged businesses. The expedited authority that is to be granted by the ICC to small businesses and minority businesses is limited to the shipment of government goods.

Aside from the issue of the effectiveness of *Ex Parte 278* in increasing the share of trucking business done by minorities, is the interesting point of why the law was needed in the first instance. Particularly insightful is the case of a black-owned trucking firm in Omaha, Nebraska. Ward Smith, the owner of the firm, submitted the low bid on a contract to ship the household goods of Offutt Air Force Base personnel. The contract was instead awarded to a white-owned trucking company that had bid $80,000 *more* than that bid by Ward Smith. Smith was denied the contract for reasons other than ability to perform the contract. He was denied the contract because he did not have state or federal authorization and was certified to move goods only within the city of Omaha.[21] Many people will suggest racial quotas and racial set-asides in government contracts to help blacks. But did Ward Smith need such help? No, he needed government off his back; he needed freedom of enterprise. Quotas as a remedy not only fail to confront the problem of government-sponsored monopolies but cause other problems. There are many *white* truckers too who, like Smith, cannot obtain certificates of authority (the Teamsters Union and the American Trucking Association seek to keep *anyone* out regardless of race). It does not do much for racial relationships if the government grants a special privilege to a black trucker and denies that special privilege to a white trucker. What the government action will do is cause conflict between black and white, who will not realize that the real culprit is government.

Union Discrimination in the Trucking Industry

The discriminatory practices of the International Brotherhood of Teamsters, the dominant union in the trucking industry, have been an important impediment to minority opportunities in trucking. Unions played a major role in getting blacks out of trucking, particularly in the South. In the post–Civil War days, trucking was regarded as a "Negro" job. As wages in the trucking industry began to rise, these jobs became attractive to whites. Today, while flagrant discrimination is not widely practiced, union work-rules penalize blacks in their advancement to the more lucrative jobs of over-the-road drivers who, in some cases, earn more than $30,000 in wage income annually.

The International Brotherhood of Teamsters negotiates seniority rules that are a part of its National Master Freight Agreement. Although there are blacks in the part of the Teamsters Union which deals in over-the-road trucking, most are dockmen and local drivers. These blacks may be high up on the seniority list, but generally over-the-road drivers are on a separate seniority list. The significance of this is that if a dockman or a local driver seeks to move to the over-the-road list, he must give up all the seniority rights he presently holds and go to the bottom of the over-the-road seniority list. Such a rule, because of the risks of unemployment and layoffs, acts as a powerful inducement not to transfer. As pointed out by attorney William B. Gould,[22] this form of seniority rules is unlawful to the extent that they adversely affect minorities.[23] According to Gould, ". . . no matter how many courts declared the provisions unlawful, the parties not directly ordered to make changes continued to adhere to the same practices and procedures."[24] Professor Gould argued that discriminatory seniority rules continue because (1) the Teamsters are a highly decentralized organization and (2) the government has been unwilling to carry its confrontation with the trucking industry to a showdown. Union officials threatened a nationwide strike if any company hired a Negro because of government pressure.

The economic impact of seniority rules struck through collective bargaining agreements is that they reduce minority opportunities to gain over-the-road trucking skills. They also perpetuate the effects of past discrimination. It perpetuates past discrimination because many trucking companies did not hire Negro road drivers until very recently.[25] Many times the Teamsters locals demanded that trucking companies practice racial employment discrimination against blacks as a condition for labor peace.[26]

Another significant factor in the problem that blacks face in their attempt to get over-the-road trucking driving positions is the refusal of white truck drivers to ride with them. The *Wall Street Journal* reported that one teamster official asked, "Would you like to climb in a bunk bed that a nigger just got out of?" Another said, "To my knowledge no law has been written yet that says a white man has to bed down with Negroes."[27] While these sentiments were expressed a few years ago, more recent evidence shows that this attitude prevails to a significant degree. This is evidenced by the fact that Teamsters Union officials protect union men who have been discharged by a company for refusing to ride with a Negro driver.[28]

Seniority rules, the refusal of white drivers to ride with Negro drivers, and highly discriminatory job referral practices by the Teamsters have contributed, and continue to contribute to reduced Negro opportunities for jobs in the trucking industry.[29]

Conclusion

For the most part piecemeal attempts to alter the institutional structure of the trucking industry have not given equality of opportunity to all potential entrants. There have been, and probably will continue to be, minor concessions here and there to assist the small businessman, particularly the minority businessman. These special exceptions to high legal entry barriers, however, come at no small personal cost to the recipient because of the legal fees and lengthy application procedures.

Complete deregulation is what is needed in the trucking industry. Deregulation will provide real equality of opportunity for all Americans in trucking. The only socially compelling regulation is in the area of truck safety. There should be three questions that should be answered satisfactorily by an applicant in order for him to operate a truck on the national roads. These are: (1) Can you drive a truck safely? (2) Is your truck safe? (3) Do you have the appropriate liability insurance? All other questions as to whether the services of the applicant are "needed" or whether he provides the "right" services will be settled by the market. If the trucker provides unneeded or wrong services, he will have few customers. He will not be able to cover all his costs. He will go bankrupt and then out of business.

Current law in the trucking industry, administered by the ICC, appears to be in violation of the spirit, if not the letter, of the Constitution of the United States.[30] Indeed, as a layman sees it, the statements of the Supreme Court of the United States would suggest that ICC restrictive practices violate the spirit of the Constitution. Justice Joseph P. Bradley (1813–92) characterized occupational freedom as an "inalienable right."[31] Justice Stephen J. Field (1816–99) said that it (occupational freedom) was a "distinguishing feature of our republican institutions."[32] Justice William O. Douglas (1898–1980) proclaimed that occupational freedom is "the most precious liberty that man possesses."[33]

It is clear that the regulation of the trucking industry does violate the democratic sentiments expressed by the several Supreme Court justices. Potential entrants are denied occupational freedom. To compound the inequity involved, the denial of occupational freedom is for the expressed purpose of protecting the incumbent trucking companies from increased competition, making their incomes higher than would otherwise be the case. The failure to recognize substantial barriers to economic opportunity has led to considerable confusion in the analysis of, and public discussion of, our nation's racial problems.

Recently there have been several suits against public policy that propose to remedy injustices against minorities. Frequently these programs seek to give minority businessmen and workers a fixed percentage of government contracts or to set hiring quotas. As such these programs have been accused of fostering what is called "reverse discrimination."

A case in point is the *Associated General Contractors of California* v. *Secretary of Commerce* (U.S.D.C., Cal. Oct. 20, 1978).[34] This case sought to enjoin the 10 percent minority set-aside provision of the Public Works Employment Act.[35] The lower court held that the set-aside for minority businessmen was unconstitutional and violated Title VI of the Civil Rights Act. On appeal the Supreme Court vacated the judgment and remanded the case, asking the lower court to consider the question of mootness.

The particular details of this case do not interest us here; however, the principles involved do. To a significant degree the difficulties that minorities face in competing for government projects are caused by government-erected barriers that impose a disproportionate burden on minorities. The difficulty that minority truckers face in getting authorization certificates is only one among many barriers erected by government. More germane to the case in point is the Davis-Bacon Act, which tends to discriminate against non-union contractors.[36] It produces a racial effect because most minority contractors are in the non-union sector.

Therefore, the set-aside program may be viewed as a remedy for the original government-mandated restriction. But it is the set-aside program that is being challenged in the courts on constitutional grounds, and the original barrier (which gives rise to minority demands for set-asides) goes completely unnoticed by the courts. In terms of equity, constitutionality and economic efficiency, the government-mandated entry restrictions would be a more suitable target. If these restrictions were to be successfully challenged and removed, there would be no necessity for the many compensatory measures that cause so much controversy in our society.

Many people clamor against quotas as a violation of democratic principles. Recently, there has been a political demand for their elimination. Those clamoring against quotas assume that the economic game is being played fairly. It is not being played fairly. It is rigged and rigged in a way particularly devastating to blacks because of their history in the United States. So the moral question has to be asked: If we are going to retain various laws and regulations that systematically discriminate against black opportunities, what do we do? If we keep the laws, then hard and fast racial quotas, in some areas, may constitute a "second-best" solution. The first-best solution, in turns of equity and efficiency, is to eliminate the regulations and eliminate the quotas.

CHAPTER 10

Economic Regulation by the States

Those who expect to reap the blessings of freedom must,
like men, undergo the fatigue of supporting it.

—Thomas Paine
The American Crisis IV
September 12, 1777

THE THESIS OF THIS BOOK is that black handicaps resulting from centuries of slavery, followed by years of gross denial of constitutional rights, have been reinforced by government laws. The government laws that have proven most devastating, for many blacks, are those that govern economic activity. The laws are not discriminatory in the sense that they are aimed specifically at blacks. But they are discriminatory in the sense that they deny full opportunity for the most disadvantaged Americans, among whom blacks are disproportionately represented.

Restrictions on the right to work are not a part of America's past value system. After all, much of the impetus for our ancestors to risk all of what they had to come to America was the search for freedom. They sought not only religious and political freedom. They sought economic freedom as well. They thought that a man should not have to get permission from the king, a mercantile association or a guild in order to pursue a particular trade. They thought that the right to work was part and parcel of the natural rights of man. What modern Americans have done is resurrect the mercantile system of monopolies and other state privileges that the Founding Fathers sought to escape.

Naturally, one asks how did we evolve from a condition of significant economic freedom to the highly restricted economic freedom of today? When we speak of economic freedom in reference to the past, we use the term with some reservation. The reason is that certain population segments, like the blacks, had little or none while others were restricted in one degree or another. But, on the other hand, there were few license requirements to practice a trade. Up until recently, there were only three licensed occupations: doctors, lawyers and ministers. Today there are more than 500 licensed occupations. Businesses were not regulated and licensed as they are today. It might be tempting to say that what's wrong with the past was all that economic freedom. But it is helpful to note that it was this period when America made its rapid growth to become a world power, all the while absorbing wave after wave of poor, illiterate immigrants from every oppressive corner of the earth.

To understand what happened to the economic freedom that did exist in America, we have to look at constitutional law. The brief review that follows will help us understand what happened. It may even suggest what can be done to bring about a larger measure of economic freedom.

A Brief Review of Constitutional Law

A leading case of the 1870s, *Munn* v. *Illinois*,[1] is typically viewed as the initial symbol of judicial deference to legislative regulation of economic activity. In this landmark decision the Supreme Court of the United States held that certain industries, "affected with a public interest," could be subjected to state regulation without violating the due process clause of the Fifth and Fourteenth amendments.[2]

Munn v. *Illinois* was one of the most far-reaching decisions of the nineteenth-century Supreme Court. It instituted state economic regulation of private businesses. In *Munn* v. *Illinois* the Court upheld an Illinois law (1873) that fixed maximum rates for grain storage. Chief Justice Waite, speaking for the majority, declared the Illinois law a legitimate expression of the police powers of the state. However,

Justice Field, in dissent, and perhaps correctly anticipating the future course of events, said, "If this be a sound law, if there be no protection either in the principles upon which our republican government is founded, or in the prohibition of the Constitution against such invasion of private rights, all property and all businesses in the State are held at the mercy of a majority of its legislature."

While the *Munn* decision made the police powers of the state to regulate private businesses explicit, it suggested potential limits on legislative powers. The Court felt that since the grain elevator operators had a virtual monopoly on grain storage, regulation of their activities was similar to the traditional rate regulation of utilities and monopolies.

In the years following the *Munn* decision, the Supreme Court moved toward substantive due process review and interpretation of state regulation.[3]

Mugler v. *Kansas*[4] signaled the Court's later interpretation of the Constitution. Justice Harlan, speaking for the Court, stated in *Mugler,* "Not every statute enacted ostensibly for the promotion of the public morals, the public health, or the public safety would be accepted as a legitimate exertion of the police powers of the State." Harlan pointed out that the courts would not be misled by mere pretenses; they were obligated to look at the substance of things.

Allgeyer v. *Louisiana*[5] marked the completion of the Court's movement to substantive due process review of state economic regulation. Allgeyer was the first case where a state law was invalidated on the ground of substantive due process. The case involved an insurance company that advertised in Louisiana but was not licensed to operate in the state. The Court's articulation of liberty of contract is what gave this case significance in the development of substantive due process, which was to influence the next thirty years of the Court's decision. Justice Peckham said:

> The liberty mentioned in that amendment [Fourteenth] means not only the right of the citizen to be free from the mere physical restraint of his person, as by incarceration, but the term is deemed to embrace the right of the citizen to be free

in the enjoyment of all of his faculties; to be free to use them in all lawful ways; to live and work where he will; to earn his livelihood by any lawful calling; to pursue any livelihood or avocation, and for that purpose to enter into all contracts which may be proper, necessary and essential to his carrying out to a successful conclusion the purposes above mentioned.[6]

The liberty of contract theme, which characterized the Court's opinion in *Allgeyer,* was to be more firmly stated in *Lochner* v. *New York.*[7] This case involved a New York State law prohibiting the employment of bakery employees for a period of more than 10 hours per day or 60 hours per week. Again Justice Peckham delivered the opinion of the Court:

The statute necessarily interferes with the right of contract between the employer and employees. . . . The general right to make a contract in relation to his business is part of the liberty of the individual protected by the Fourteenth Amendment of the Federal Constitution. The right to purchase or sell labor is part of the liberty protected by this amendment, unless there are circumstances which exclude the right. . . . This court has recognized the existence and upheld the exercise of the police powers of the States in many cases which might fairly be considered border ones. . . . It must, of course, be conceded that there is a limit to the valid exercise of the police power by the State. . . . Otherwise the Fourteenth Amendment would have no efficacy and the legislatures of the States would have unbounded power, and it would be enough to say that any piece of legislation was enacted to conserve the morals, the health or safety of the people; such legislation would be valid, no matter how absolutely without foundation the claim might be. The claim of the police power would be a mere pretext—become another and delusive name for the Supreme Sovereignty of the State to be exercised free from constitutional restraint.[8]

From the *Lochner* decision until the mid-1930s, the Supreme Court held unconstitutional many state laws that regulated economic activity on substantive due process grounds. Many of the state laws that were struck down were those regulating product prices and labor wages, including those fixing minimum wages, and especially vulnerable during this period were laws regulating conditions for entering into business. In studying this period, an economist would see that the Court struck down, as unconstitutional, many state laws providing the mechanism for producer collusions.[9]

Thus, in numerous decisions prior to 1937, the U.S. Supreme Court ruled that the liberty guaranteed by the due process clause included the liberty to contract. The basic restriction, narrowly interpreted, was in businesses "affected with the public interest." Government infringement on basic economic relationships such as wages and prices was held to be a violation of the Fifth and Fourteenth amendments.[10] The due process clause was interpreted as barring both state and federal governments from regulating businesses not affected with the public interest.

Numerous attempts by states were made to circumvent court rulings. Of particular interest is the *New State Ice Co.* v. *Liebman*[11] because of its similarities to current practices in truck and taxi regulation. In this case the Supreme Court invalidated an Oklahoma law that treated ice manufacturing as a public utility, i.e., an activity affected with the public interest. The Oklahoma law required, as a condition of entry, that public "need and convenience" be demonstrated before one could manufacture ice. The burden of proving public need and necessity, i.e., that there were not enough existing facilities to meet public demand, was on the prospective entrant. The Court held that such licensure was an invalid regulation of a business not affected with a public interest and a denial of liberty to pursue a lawful calling contrary to the due process clause of the Fourteenth Amendment.

In dissenting, Justice Brandeis expressed an opinion that was to be adopted by the Court in later years: "The notion of a distinct category of business 'affected with the public interest' employing property 'devoted to a public use' rests upon historical error. In my opinion the true principle is that the State's power extends for the public protection. I find in the due process clause no other limitation upon the character and scope or regulation permissible."[12]

A 1934 case, *Nebbia* v. *New York,* marks the break in the U.S. Supreme Court's distinction between "businesses affected with the public interests" and any other kind of business.[13] *Nebbia* protested against the New York State law that fixed the minimum price of milk at the retail level. *Nebbia* claimed that price regulation by the state, except in business affecting the public interest such as utilities— for example, railroads, water and electricity—was a violation of the due process clause of the Constitution. The Court did not agree. The Court declared that there is "no closed category of business affected with the public interest." Justice Roberts, speaking for the majority, said:

> The Fifth Amendment, in the field of Federal activity, and the Fourteenth, as respects state action, do not prohibit governmental regulation for the public welfare. They merely condition the execution of the admitted power, by securing that the end shall be accomplished by methods consistent with due process . . . demands only that the law shall not be unreasonable, arbitrary, or capricious, and that the means selected shall have a real and substantial relation to the object sought to be attained.[14]

But Justice Reynolds, dissenting with the majority in *Nebbia,* held that:

> This is not regulation, but management, control, dictation— it amounts to the deprivation of the fundamental right which one has to conduct his own affairs honestly and along customary lines . . . if it be now ruled that one dedicates his property to public use whenever he embarks on an enterprise which the Legislature may think is desirable to bring under control, this is but to declare that rights guaranteed by the Constitution exist only so long as supposed public interest does not require their extinction. To adopt such a view, of course, would put an end to liberty under the Constitution.[15]

Essentially then, during the decades preceding *Nebbia,* the constitutional issue of a state's economic regulation within its borders was resolved. The states were held to pass only those laws that have a "reasonable and proper" legislative purpose and are neither discriminatory nor arbitrary. *Nebbia* was to usher in a different Court attitude. In 1937 the shift in the Court's interpretation of the Constitution was sealed. In *West Coast Hotel* v. *Parrish*[16] the Court upheld the validity of the Washington State minimum wage law and thereby rejected its own principles enunciated in the *Adkins*[17] case. It upheld the National Labor Relations Act and the Railway Labor Act,[18] both requiring that employers bargain with union representatives who were chosen by a majority of employees. Both of these decisions stand in stark contrast with the Court's earlier decisions, most notably in *Adair* v. *United States*[19] and *Coppage* v. *Kansas.*[20]

During this period the Court effectively ruled out liberty of contract as a guarantee of the Fifth and Fourteenth amendments and substituted procedural due process as the criterion for judging the constitutionality of state exercise of its police powers. *West Coast Hotel* v. *Parrish*[21] is thought of as the watershed case in the Court's interpretation of the Constitution. In *West Coast Hotel,* a case challenging the constitutionality of the Washington State minimum wage law, Chief Justice Hughes overruled the earlier *Adkins* v. *Children's Hospital* decision. In the *Adkins* case, Justice Sutherland said that freedom of contract was the general rule and restraint the exception. He also pointed out that since the Nineteenth Amendment, women were not civilly inferior and hence liberty of contract could not be subject to greater restriction for women than for men (the *Adkins* case concerned a minimum wage law for *women only* in the District of Columbia). Contrast Chief Justice Hughes's opinion for the majority in *West Coast* (also a minimum wage law for women):

> What can be closer to the public interest than the health of women and their protection from unscrupulous and over-reaching employers? And if the protection of women is a legitimate end of the exercise of state power, how can it be said that the requirement of the payment of a minimum wage

fairly fixed in order to meet the very necessities of existence is not an admissible means to that end? . . . Our conclusion is that the case of *Adkins v. Children's Hospital,* supra, should be, and it is, overruled.

The dissenting justices, in a 5 to 4 decision, said:

Neither the statute involved in the *Adkins* case nor the Washington statute . . . has the slightest relation to the capacity or earning power of the employee. . . . The sole basis upon which the question of validity rests is the assumption that the employee is entitled to receive a sum of money sufficient to provide a living for her, keep her in health and preserve her morals. . . . The law takes account of the necessities of only one party to the contract. It ignores the necessities of the employer by compelling him to pay not less than a certain sum, not only whether the employee is capable of earning it, but irrespective of the ability of his business to sustain the burden. . . . To the extent that the sum fixed exceeds the fair value of the services rendered, it amounts to a compulsory exaction from the employer for the support of a partially indigent person . . . it arbitrarily shifts to his shoulders a burden which, if it belongs to anybody, belongs to society as a whole. . . .

Hughes said that an employer should pay an hourly wage that will meet "the very necessities of existence" of the worker. The dissent points out that such a sum may exceed the value of some employee's services. If the employer hires such a worker, the law requires the payment of a gift to the worker. Of course employers will attempt to avoid paying a gift. One way is not to hire the worker whose services do not equal or exceed the mandated wage. The justices in dissent are really saying that the burden of an indigent worker is not that of the employer but that of society. In this sense they might have insightfully provided the moral argument for the "negative income tax." This idea was proposed by Professor Milton Friedman some years ago. Essentially it says that a person should be allowed to earn whatever wage he can. If society deems that the income thereby generated is insufficient, an automatic payment from the Treasury to make up the difference would be forth-coming.

A year after *West Coast,* Justice Stone, for the Court, went further down the road toward striking down a substantive due process interpretation of the Constitution in *United States* v. *Carolene Products.*[22] Justice Stone, in this case, held that state economic regulation, even in businesses not affected with the public interest, *is* constitutional as long as the regulatory legislation rests upon some rational basis.

At least at this point of constitutional history, a regulatory law could be declared unconstitutional by proving that the law had no rational basis. But by 1941, even this requirement was abandoned. In *Olsen* v. *Nebraska,* the state courts had held as unconstitutional a law fixing maximum employment-agency fees.[23] The Supreme Court unanimously reversed. Justice Douglas, speaking for the Court, said that the state did not have to prove that a regulatory law was appropriate: "Differences of opinion on that score suggest a choice which should be left where . . . it was left by the Constitution—to the State and to Congress."[24]

In Supreme Court decisions that followed, the Court's attitude was made clear. In the *Day-Brite* v. *Missouri*[25-26] decision, Justice Douglas, speaking for the Court, held that it was not for the Supreme Court to decide whether regulatory legislation "offends the public welfare."[27] In the *Williamson* v. *Lee Optical Company* decision, the Court reiterated its stance. In this case the Court upheld a state law requiring a prescription before an optician could fit old lenses to new frames; the Court said that even though the law may cause "needless, wasteful requirement in most cases," the legislature "might have concluded" that such waste was justified in order to protect public health.[28]

There is considerable speculation attempting to explain the extraordinary shift in the Court's judicial values. The strongest contender is that the "extremism" of the Court in the pre–1937 years, which saw a strong resistance to economic experimentation, typified by its anti–New Deal decisions, gave rise to extremism in another direction through those who thought that government should play a larger role in the conduct of economic affairs.[29] Another explanation for the Court's departure from substantive due process interpretation of the Constitution is that the Court mirrors public opinion. This is seen in Justice Holmes's opinion in the *Tyson* case: "The truth seems to me to be that, subject to compensation when compensation is due, *the legislature may forbid or restrict any business when it has a sufficient force of public opinion behind it.*"[30] At the time of the *Tyson* case, those justices opposed to constitutional laissez-faire were in the minority; in later years those justices constituted the majority on the Court.

Essentially in the late 1930s and the 1940s and thereafter, the Courts made the interpretation that state economic regulation was not a violation of the guarantees of the Fifth and Fourteenth amendments. Further, they made it clear that it was not their job to question the rationality or wisdom of state economic regulation. They held that it was within the police powers of the state to pursue economic regulation and economic experimentation.

To the legal layman the position of the Courts borders on the unbelievable. Imagine a would-be barber, a would-be taxicab owner or a would-be real estate broker who has been denied entry because of state regulation, which protects existing practitioners from competition, successfully waging a political campaign against the entrenched, monied barber, taxi and real estate broker interests in the state capitol. Justice Douglas, perhaps recognizing that state occupational licensing gives the state an opportunity for arbitrary action, said:

> The right to work, I had assumed, was the most precious liberty that man possesses. Man has indeed as much right to work as he has to live, to be free, to own property. . . . To work means to eat. It means also to live. For many it would be better to work in a jail, than to sit idle on the curb. The great values of freedom are in the opportunities afforded man to press to new horizons, to pit his strength against the forces of nature, to match skills with his fellow man.[31]

Such sentiments have always characterized Court rhetoric. Justice Bradley viewed occupational freedom as an "inalienable right."[32] Occupational freedom was viewed by Justice Field as a "distinguishing feature of our republican institutions."[33] Justice Rufus W. Peckman (1838–1909) said, "The liberty mentioned in that Amendment (Fourteenth) means . . . to earn his livelihood by any lawful calling; to pursue any livelihood or avocation. . . ."[34]

Despite these traditional pronouncements, occupational freedom has little meaning as demonstrated by contemporary Court opinion. Contrast Mr. Justice Douglas's statement (above) with his statement just one year later in a case involving a plaintiff whose occupational choice was restricted by the state:

The day is gone when this court uses the Due Process Clause of the Fourteenth Amendment to strike down state laws, regulatory of business and industrial conditions, because they may be unwise, improvident, or out of harmony with a particular school of thought. . . . We emphasize again what Chief Justice Waite said in *Munn v. Illinois,* 94 U.S. 113, 134, "For protections against abuses by the legislatures people must resort to the polls, not to the courts."[35]

Justice Douglas reiterated the fact that individual occupational freedom was secondary to state convenience:

Our recent decisions make plain that we do not sit as a super-legislature to weigh the wisdom of legislation nor to decide whether the policy which it expresses offends the public welfare. The legislative power has limits. . . . But the state legislatures have constitutional authority to experiment with new techniques; they are entitled to their own standard of the public welfare; they may within extremely broad limits control practices in the business-labor field, so long as specific constitutional prohibitions are not violated and so long as conflicts with valid and controlling federal laws are avoided.[36]

By the time of *Ferguson* v. *Skrupa,* in 1963, substantive due process as a restriction of state regulation of economic activity was, without question, dead. In holding valid a Kansas law that made it a misdemeanor for a person to engage in debt adjustment without being a Kansas-licensed lawyer, Justice Black said:

> We have returned to the original constitutional proposition that courts do not substitute their social and economic beliefs for the judgment of legislative bodies, who are elected to pass laws. . . . The Kansas debt adjusting statute may be wise or unwise. But relief, if any be needed, lies not with us but with the body constituted to pass laws for the State of Kansas.[37]

Therefore, the Court, through most of its post-1940 decisions, has entrusted basic individual rights having to do with economic freedom of contract to the legislatures of the states. On the other hand, the Court has been ambivalent in reaching decisions where economic freedom of contract *and* freedom of speech issues simultaneously present themselves. For example, in *Barsky* v. *Board of Regents,*[38] the petitioner had "left wing" connections that led to the licensing authority's revocation of his physician's license. The Court sustained the revocation against the charge of unreasonableness, whim and caprice even though the evidence that such was the case was fairly strong.[39] In *Barsky,* Justices Black, Frankfurter and Douglas dissented, emphasizing that the conduct constituting the crime had no bearing on the appellant's competency to practice medicine.

However, just a few years later the Court held invalid a similar restraint on occupational freedom. In this case, *Schware* v. *Board of Examiners,*[40] the petitioner had been denied permission to take the state bar examination on the ground that he did not meet the "good moral character" requirement of the state. The New Mexico board had refused to let Schware take the state bar because of his former association with subversive groups and his record of arrest. Justice Black, for the Court, in invalidating the state's claim, said:

> We need not enter into a discussion whether the practice of law is a "right" or "privilege." Regardless of how the State's

grant of permission to engage in this occupation is characterized, it is sufficient to say that a person cannot be prevented
from practicing except for valid reasons. Certainly the practice of law is not a matter of the State's grace.[41]

Justice Black, delivering the opinion for the Court, said
that state occupational qualifications must have a rational
basis connected with the fitness or capacity of the candidate
to perform the occupation.[42]

The history of Supreme Court interpretation of constitutional law demonstrates the difficulty, at least for the layman, of interpreting the Court's translation of guarantees
found in the U.S. Bill of Rights. In addition, one places him-
self in considerable jeopardy if he attempts to derive general
principles from *one* Court opinion to use as predictors of
future Court opinions, even when the Court membership
does not change.

Take the declaration by Mr. Justice Black speaking for
the Court in *Schware*. Black said that state-imposed qualifications "must have a rational connection with the applicant's fitness or capacity" to practice the occupation.[43]
Clearly, if a literal interpretation is given to Justice Black's
declaration, it would appear that there would be many forms
of economic regulation at the state or local levels which
the Court would hold as invalid exercise of the police powers
of the state. For example, the City of New York requires
the possession of a medallion for each taxi that operates
within the city. Because the city has not issued a new medallion since 1937, the only way that one can be obtained is
through the purchase of an *existing* medallion, which has
a current price of about $60,000. Therefore, the city, through
its numerical restriction on medallions, causes a new entrant to pay $60,000 as a condition of entry. Such a require-
ment or qualification has no "rational connection with the
applicant's fitness or capacity" to practice the occupation,
i.e., to own a taxi and provide taxi services. As we have
pointed out earlier, the entry conditions in Washington, D.C.,
have a more nearly rational basis for state regulation of
economic activity. The District of Columbia Public Services

Commission requires that the applicant certify his vehicle as being safe (inspected) and that he have a minimum amount of liability insurance in force and a chauffeur's license. The right to own and operate a taxi, itself, costs an annual fee of $25!

Possible Challenges to State Economic Regulation

As this brief history of economic regulation has shown, there is little basis for optimism about a successful challenge on constitutional principles. The only limitation that the Court has placed on state economic regulation is that it may not act in an arbitrary, capricious or unreasonable manner in the exercise of its police powers. However, these limitations do not get us very far in the specification of the precise bounds of state intervention into the economic arena because "arbitrary," "capricious" and "unreasonable" mean different things to different people at different times.

Title VII of the Civil Rights Act, and the cases that have arisen under it, may constitute a basis for the challenge of some forms of economic regulation. Section 703(h) of Title VII says that it shall not be an unlawful employment practice:

> . . . for an employer to give and to act upon the results of any professionally developed ability test provided such a test, its administration or action upon the results is not designed, intended, or used to discriminate because of race, color, religion, sex, or national origin. . . .

Therefore, testing procedures are lawful within the meaning of the Civil Rights Act only if they can be shown to be job-related.

Griggs v. *Duke Power Company* was a major case arising under Title VII of the Civil Rights Act of 1964.[44] The lower court found that the high school and test requirements for employee promotion and assignment had been adopted without any discriminatory intent against Negro employees. But Chief Justice Burger, speaking for a unanimous Court, declared that "good intent or absence of discriminatory intent does not redeem employment procedures or testing mechanisms that operate as 'built-in headwinds' for minority groups and are unrelated to measuring job capability. . . . Congress directed the thrust of the act to the *consequences* of employment practices, not simply the motivation. More than that, Congress has placed on the employer the burden of showing that any given requirement must have a manifest relationship to the employment in question." Justice Burger stated further: ". . . The Act proscribes not only overt discrimination but also practices that are fair in form, but discriminatory in operation. The touchstone is business necessity. If an employment practice which operates to exclude Negroes cannot be shown to be related to job performance, the practice is prohibited."

Again, if one literally applied the Court's opinion to the ownership of taxis or trucks as a form of employment, albeit self-employment, he would find the entry requirements to be invalid. That is, the ability to purchase expensive licenses to own and operate a truck or taxi does not appear to be a requirement that is necessary for the performance of the service in question. Further, even though discriminatory racial intent cannot be shown as a basis for taxi licenses or Interstate Commerce Commission certificates of authorization, preliminary evidence shows that the *consequence* is that of barring entry, particularly for disadvantaged minorities. In the case of Interstate Commerce Commission certificates of authority, the case is quite clear. Virtually all the more than 16,000 certificates of authority were issued in 1935 after the enactment of the Motor Carrier Act. At that time, blacks did not have trucks in any number, much less the constitutional guarantees that they possess today. In effect, the certification process tends to make permanent the historical disadvantages of blacks in the trucking business. It is in this sense—equity considerations—that it can be shown that a good bit of economic regulation at the state, federal and local levels is violative of the Civil Rights Act of 1964 and the Equal Protection Clause of the Constitution.

Some recent challenges to economic regulation have

come in the form of antitrust suits by the Department of Justice and the Federal Trade Commission. The Antitrust Division of the Justice Department has taken the American Bar Association and the Texas State Board of Public Accountants to court charging violations of federal antitrust laws. The Federal Trade Commission is now conducting investigations into licensing "to identify instances of disguised monopoly." Furthermore, the Equal Employment Opportunity Commission is now contending that job discrimination by state licensing boards violates Title VII of the 1964 Civil Rights Act. In addition, Congress, as a result of trucking deregulation legislation, is conducting studies into the monopoly aspects of Interstate Commerce Commission administrative law.

CHAPTER 11

Conclusion

Premum Non Nocere

—*Hippocratic Oath*

THE THEME THROUGHOUT THIS book is that racial antipathy and discrimination do not explain all that they are purported to explain. The fact that a person *likes* one race over another does not tell us what that person will find to be in his interests. This is just as true as in the case of anything else. Knowledge that some people like Rolls-Royces better than Pintos or twenty-five-point diamonds better than two-point diamonds, alone, cannot unambiguously tell us which the person will possess. To understand fully what people will in fact do, one not only needs to know what people desire, one also needs to know the costs that people must pay for the desired object in question.

All economic evidence shows that the lower the cost of doing something, the more people will do it. Very often the government lowers the costs involved. When the government fixes prices, wages, profits or rents, the tendency for choices to be made on noneconomic criteria increases. Race, sex, national origin are all noneconomic criteria. The chapters on the railroad industry and on minimum wages demonstrated how wage-fixing has heightened the disadvantages faced by blacks.

The reason why blacks are disadvantaged because of government intervention is no mystery. There is a kind of parity in the marketplace that does not exist in the political arena. Discriminated-against people generally do better under a system where there is market allocation of goods and services than when there is political allocation of goods and services. The market resembles one-man-one-vote. This means that one person's one dollar is the same as another person's one dollar. The difference between people lies in the number of dollars they have. No such parity exists in the political arena.

When choices are made in the market arena, people, including poor people, have a higher probability of getting *some* of what they want, even if they are a minority. When choices are made through the political arena, they very well may get *none* of what they want. That is, if the majority votes to use social resources to produce X and the minority voted for Y, if majority rule carries the day, there will be no Y.

Partial evidence of this, as Dr. Milton Friedman points out, is seen in the poorest ghettos of the nation.[1] If you go through the ghetto, you will see *some* nice cars, *some* nice clothing and *some* nice foods. In that respect the residents have *some* of the things that middle-class and rich people possess. But you will see no nice public schools. Why not at least *some* public schools like rich people have? Cars, clothing and food are distributed by the market mechanism. Schools are distributed by the political mechanism. More often than not, if a nice school is found in the ghetto, it is a nonpublic school.

The power of the market is seen when one looks at the historical housing opportunities for blacks. Appreciation of the market ability to thwart the forces of racial discrimination is gained by asking the following question: How did blacks seize the use-control of housing in the central areas of most major cities? During the racially hostile times of the 1920s, 30s, 40s, one could not prevent whole blocks and neighborhoods from going from white to black virtually overnight. That fact ought to give rise to the question: How did poor, discriminated-against blacks do this? Keep in mind that some of these neighborhoods were occupied by relatively affluent whites.

The poor blacks simply outbid the whites for the property. At first thought, the ability of poor people to outbid nonpoor people may seem an impossibility. But an example can show how it is possible. Imagine a three-story brownstone being rented by a nonpoor white family for $200 per month. Suppose further that the landlord does not like blacks. But if six poor black families suggested that the building be partitioned into six parts to rent for $75 per part, the landlord might have to reassess his position. Namely, he would have to evaluate the prospect of an income yield of $450, by renting to the six blacks, as opposed to an income yield of $200 by retaining his white tenant. The fact that blacks have come to occupy neighborhoods formerly occupied by whites demonstrates that the landlord's dilemma was resolved in favor of blacks.

Now the question: Why is it that poor blacks did not inundate suburban areas to the extent they did the cities? The answer is easy: The power of the state subverted the operation of the market. Suburban areas, to a greater extent than cities, have highly restrictive zoning ordinances. There are laws that fix the minimum lot size, minimum floor space in the house, minimum distance to adjacent houses plus laws that restrict property use to a single family. The combined effect of these laws, independent of *de jure* or *de facto* racial discrimination, is to deny poor people the chance to outbid nonpoor people. It is far more difficult for a person to get together the whole house price than one month's rent for a cubbyhole.

Herein lies the power of the market. People can offset some of their handicaps by offering a higher price for what they buy or a lower price for what they sell. Many well-meaning people are morally outraged by such a necessity. But the fact of business is that if handicapped people are not permitted to use price as a bargaining tool, they may very well end up with none of what they want as opposed to some.[2]

There are numerous laws, regulations and ordinances that have reduced or eliminated avenues of upward mobility for blacks. The common feature of these barriers is that they prevent people from making transactions that are deemed mutually beneficial by the *transactors.* However, it would be extremely misleading to leave the reader with the impression that these laws are exclusively antiblack. An ordinance that generates a $60,000 license price to own a taxi, such as the one in New York City, discriminates and handicaps *anyone,* brown, black, white or yellow, who cannot meet the price. Therefore, these laws are antipeople! They are only antiblack to the extent that blacks may be least likely to meet the entry conditions. Blacks were the last major ethnic group to become urbanized and to gain basic civil rights. When they finally achieved that status, blacks found that new barriers had been erected.

Laws that restrict economic activity are antipeople in another way. Another effect of these laws is they *always* raise prices and often reduce the received quality of the regulated good or service. This makes for a lower standard of living than would be the case with less restrictive licensing and regulation. On top of this, American citizens are made to suffer in two additional ways. Because of restricted economic opportunities more people than otherwise would be the case are living at taxpayer expense through welfare, unemployment compensation and other income supplemental programs. Moreover, when we are called to support the indigent the support level is higher because of the higher product prices caused by the monopolistic restrictions.

Our recognition that laws which create economic barriers are antipeople is important, not for analytical clarity alone, but for another reason as well. Such a recognition may suggest political strategy for change. The people who financially benefit from New York's taxicab monopoly, for example, are relatively few in number. The beneficiaries are taxi owners and those in allied trades. The people who bear the burden of the monopoly are large in number. They are the taxicab riders of New York City, who receive a lower quality service and pay higher prices, and all those who would enter the taxi business.

Such a tabulation of beneficiaries and losers of New York's taxi monopoly suggests that a political coalition could be formed to eliminate the monopoly. A coalition of voters could be formed to counter the political pressure by the Teamsters Union and taxi owner associations to maintain and enhance the monopoly. Moreover, the recognition that government-sponsored monopolies are antipeople tells us that blacks, who are already taxi owners, are part of the opposition. People like a monopoly in what they sell. Black people are not immune to this propensity. Blacks who are a part of a monopolized market structure, such as a licensed trade or occupation or a union-protected job, will share the same interest in monopoly maintenance as whites.

Economically the solution to problems of upward mobility that blacks face are relatively simple. Their most difficult problem lies in the political arena. How can they eliminate or reduce the power of interest groups to use government to exclude? The broad solution to exclusion for all Americans is for the United States Supreme Court to interpret the right to work as it now interprets the right to speech. The Court has all but said that there is no compelling state reason for limiting freedom of speech. Similarly, there are very few compelling state reasons for limiting the freedom to work.

It is hoped that this book will help sift through much of the nonsense that is being said about black economic progress so that national resources can be more effectively focused on the true causal factors.

NOTES

CHAPTER 1

1. See U.S. Bureau of Census, *Current Population Reports,* P-60, No. 85, December 1972.

2. Lester C. Thurow, *Poverty and Discrimination* (Washington, D.C.: The Brookings Institution, 1969), p. 2.

3. This is essentially the position taken by those who advocate "ghetto dispersal." See John F. Kain and Joseph J. Persky, "Alternative to the Gilded Ghetto," *The Public Interest* (winter 1969), pp. 74–87.

4. Anthony Downs, *Urban Problems and Prospects* (Chicago: Markham Publishing Co., 1970), p. 76.

5. Ibid., p. 96.

6. Daniel R. Fusfeld, *The Basic Economics of the Urban Racial Crisis* (New York: Holt, Rinehart & Winston, Inc., 1973), pp. 115–16.

7. For an excellent discussion of immigrant groups see: Oscar Handlin, *The Uprooted* (New York: Grosset & Dunlap, 1951); J.C. Furnas, *The Americans* (New York: G.P. Putnam's Sons, 1969); Nathan Glazer and Daniel Patrick Moynihan, *Beyond the Melting Pot* (Cambridge, Mass.: MIT Press, 1963).

8. Bob Hepple, *Race, Jobs and the Law in Britain,* 2nd ed. (London: Penguin Books, Ltd., 1970), p. 20 ff.

9. R.A. Schermerhorn, *Comparative Ethnic Relations* (New York: Random House, 1970), p. 75.

10. Yosh Tandon, *Problems of a Displaced Minority: The New Position of East Africa's Asians* (London: Minority Rights Group, 1972), p. 5.

11. The ironic aspect of this whole matter was that anti-Asian feelings developed even in light of Indian support and collaboration with the Africans in their struggles for independence. The Indians

considered Mau Mau as an orthodox struggle and were sympathetic to its aims; Indian newspapers voiced Black African opinion and directly sponsored publication of their newspapers, assisted in African education and were in general cooperative with the East Africans. But none of this overshadowed the rising intensity of African nationalism and the resentment by the Africans of the Indian socioeconomic position in the territories. See J.S. Mangat, *A History of the Asians in East Africa* (London: Oxford University Press, 1969), esp. pp. 172–78.

12. Ibid., p. 15 ff.

13. In Uganda, in addition to the expulsion of Asians, there has been a mass execution of the Langi and the Acholi by the Nubians. See John Humphreys, "Amin Promises Liberation, Delivers Exile and Murder," *Matchbox* (spring/summer 1975), pp. 7–12.

14. Except in Burma, where the Indians are even more despised.

15. Hugh Mabbett, *The Chinese in Indonesia, the Philippines and Malaysia* (London: Minority Rights Group, 1972), p. 19, 24.

16. Ibid., p. 5.

17. See T.H. Silcock, "The Effects of Industrialization on Race Relations in Malaya," in *Industrialization and Race Relations,* ed., Guy Hunter (New York: Oxford University Press, 1965), pp. 177–200.

18. See Virginia Thompson and Richard Adloff, *Minority Problems in Southeast Asia* (Stanford: Stanford University Press, 1955); G.W. Skinner, *Leadership and Power in the Chinese Community of Thailand* (Ithaca, N.Y.: Cornell University Press, 1958).

19. Hugh Mabbett, *The Chinese,* p. 25.

20. We might add that in the East African states of Kenya, Tanzania and Uganda, before Asian expulsion, the Indians representing an alien and politically powerless yet economically powerful middle class owned large industrial enterprises and controlled most of the retail activity. They are discriminated against by both the Africans and the Europeans. See: Yash Tandon, *Problems of a Displaced Minority: The New Position of East Africa's Asians* (London: Minority Rights Group, 1972).

21. Some observers of the Chinese problem in southeast Asia assert that the resentment and hostility against the alien Chinese population is caused by their success in the economic sphere. Con-

trast this assertion with that frequently made with regard to ethnic minorities in the United States, that they are unsuccessful in the economic sphere because of white hostility and resentment.

22. Thomas Sowell, *Race and Economics* (New York: David McKay Co., Inc., 1975), p. 127.

23. William Petersen, "Chinese and Japanese Americans," in *Essays and Data on American Ethnic Groups,* ed., Thomas Sowell (Washington, D.C.: The Urban Institute, 1978), pp. 65–106.

24. U.S. Department of Labor, Bureau of Labor Statistics, "Asian Americans in the Labor Market," *Monthly Labor Review* (July 1975), pp. 33–38.

25. One argument that may be given for the relative ease of compliance with the law is that the duration of contact between buyer and seller is short and the seller is likely to move out of the neighborhood.

26. Whenever there is a disparity between the personal values of goods for any two persons, exchange possibilities exist that will permit each person to achieve a higher level of satisfaction.

27. For a theoretical discussion of this phenomenon see Charles M. Tiebout, "A Pure Theory of Local Expenditures," *Journal of Political Economy,* LXIV (October 1956), pp. 416–24; Yoram Barzel, "Two Propositions on the Optimum Level of Producing Collective Goods," *Public Choice,* 6 (spring 1969), pp. 31–37; Robert L. Bish and Hugh O. Nourse, *Urban Economics and Policy Analysis* (New York: McGraw-Hill Book Co., 1975), pp. 129–31.

28. Reynolds Farley, "Suburban Persistence," *American Sociological Review* (February 1964), p. 47. See also: Charles S. Benson and Peter B. Lund, *Neighborhood Distribution of Local Public Services* (Berkeley: Institute of Governmental Studies, 1969).

29. In a report, *Building the American City* (Washington, D.C.: Government Printing Office, 1969), p. 149, the U.S. National Commission on Urban Problems (The Douglas Commission) states the following: ". . . These latter purposes were not explicitly avowed but were soon detected. Those who were generally hostile to racial integration were therefore successful in persuading the House to require that the consent of a locality was necessary before rent supplements could be put into effect there. Unfortunately, this virtually barred the program from the suburbs." Earlier in the report, it was conceded, however, that economic class antagonisms played some role in suburban rejection of low-income housing.

30. See Ben J. Wattenberg, *The Real America* (New York: Doubleday & Co., Inc., 1974), pp. 244–45.

31. Thomas F. Peltigrew, "Attitude on Race and Housing: A Social-Psychological View" in *Segregation in Residential Areas,* (eds.) Amos H. Hawley and Vincent P. Rock (Washington, D.C.: National Academy of Sciences, 1973), pp. 21–84.

32. Contrast these findings with, for example, such misleading statements as: "Most whites simply do not want Negroes living next door or in white neighborhoods." See L.W. Eley and T.S. Casstevens, *The Politics of Fair Housing Legislation: State and Local Case Studies* (San Francisco: Chandler Publishers, 1968), pp. 6–7.

33. See *New York Times* (July 24, 1970), p. 27.

34. See Nathan Glazer, *Affirmative Discrimination* (New York: Basic Books, Inc., 1975), pp. 160–64.

35. See "Black Middleclass Joining the Exodus to White Suburbia," *New York Times* (Jan. 4, 1976), p. 1 and p. 40.

36. The number of blacks living in suburbs between 1970 and 1974 has increased by 550,000, more than 11 percent of the net (4,600,000) migration to the suburbs. See U.S. Department of Commerce, Bureau of Census, *Current Population Reports,* Series P-23, No. 55, "Social and Economic Characteristics of the Metropolitan and Non-Metropolitan Population: 1974–1970." (Washington, D.C.: Government Printing Office, 1975), p. 1.

37. Obviously, the movement by middle-class blacks has the same center city fiscal implications as that of movement by white middle-class families: each erodes the city tax base.

38. Leo F. Schnore, "Social Class Segregation Among Nonwhites in Metropolitan Centers," *Demography* (1965), 2, pp. 126–33.

39. Leo F. Schnore, "Social Classes in Cities and Suburbs," in *Segregation in Residential Areas,* (eds.) Amos H. Hawley and Vincent P. Rock (Washington, D.C.: National Academy of Sciences, 1973), pp. 199.

40. 418 U.S. 717 (1974).

41. 373 F. Supp. 208 (N.D. Ill., 1973).

42. See Gregory A. Adamski and Stephen B. Engleman, "Civil Rights and Civil Liberties," *Chicago Kent Law Review,* Vol. 32, No. 2 (1975), pp. 246–93.

43. *Hills, Secretary of Housing and Urban Development* v. *Dorothy Gatreaux* et al., 425 U.S. 284 (1976).

CHAPTER 2

1. This is not completely true: one report estimates that approximately 2,600 Negroes become white, "pass," each year. See E.W. Eckard, "How Many Negroes Pass?," *American Journal of Sociology* (May 1947), pp. 498–500.

2. It is important to recognize the difference between causality and correlation. The rooster crowing is correlated with the sunrise, but is not the cause of the sunrise. However, if one has to predict the sunrise, the crowing of the rooster is a good predictor.

3. Walter E. Williams, "Some Hard Questions on Minority Businesses," *Negro Educational Review* (April/July 1974), pp. 123–42; Andrew F. Brimmer, "The Black Banks: An Assessment of Performance and Prospect." *The Journal of Finance* (May 1971), pp. 379–405.

4. See David Caplovitz, *The Poor Pay More* (New York: Free Press of Glencoe, 1967); Warren G. Magnuson and Jean Carter, *The Dark Side of the Market Place* (Englewood Cliffs, N.J.: Prentice-Hall, Inc., 1968); Frederick Sturdivant, "Better Deal for Ghetto Shoppers," *Harvard Business Review* (March–April 1968), pp. 130–39; Frederick Sturdivant and Walter Wilhelm, "Poverty, Minorities and Consumer Exploitation," *Social Science Quarterly* (December 1968), pp. 643–50.

5. Federal Trade Commission, *Economic Report on Installment Credit and Retail Sales Practices of District of Columbia Retailers* (Washington, D.C.: Government Printing Office, 1968).

CHAPTER 3

1. The role and actions of businessmen are largely misconceived by Americans victimized by antibusiness ideology. The businessman, in the literal sense of the word, is really an employee. Customers, acting collectively, are the employers. The fact that customers exhibit preferences for lower prices forces the businessman to make adjustments that minimize production costs, given a rise in labor prices. If he does not make adjustments, he will lose his customers and/or investors to those firms who do make

the corresponding adjustments. These cost-minimizing adjustments would be unnecessary were his customers indifferent to prices.

2. Actually the cost to the employer is higher because, in addition to wages, he pays fringe benefits such as Social Security, medical insurance and the like.

3. It is important to note that most people acquire work skills by working at a "subnormal wage," which amounts to the same thing as paying to learn. For example, inexperienced doctors (interns), during their training, work at wages which are a tiny fraction of that of trained doctors. College students forego considerable amounts of money in the form of tuition and foregone income so that they may develop marketable skills. It is ironic, if not tragic, that low-skilled youths from poor families are denied an opportunity to get a start in life. This is exactly what happens when a high minimum wage forbids low-skilled workers to pay for job training in the form of a lower beginning wage. It must be remembered that teenagers are not supporting families and in most cases are living at home and hence could afford to "pay" for their training.

4. See David E. Haun, "Minimum Wages, Factor Substitution, and the Marginal Producer," *Quarterly Journal of Economics* (August 1965), pp. 478–86; Yale Brozen, "The Effect of Statutory Minimum Wages on Teenage Unemployment," *Journal of Law and Economics* (April 1969), pp. 109–22; Marvin Kosters and Finis Welch, "The Effects of Minimum Wages on the Distribution of Changes in Aggregate Employment," *American Economic Review* (June 1972), pp. 323–32; William G. Bowen and T. Aldrich Finegan, *The Economics of Labor Force Participation* (Princeton University Press, 1969); Edmund S. Phelps, *Inflationary Policy and Unemployment Theory* (New York: W.W. Norton and Co., 1972); Arthur F. Burns, *The Management of Prosperity* (New York: Columbia University Press, 1966); Thomas G. Moore, "The Effect of Minimum Wages on Teenage Unemployment Rates," *Journal of Political Economy* (July/August 1971), pp. 897–902; James F. Ragan, Jr., "Minimum Wages and the Youth Labor Market," *The Review of Economics and Statistics* (May 1977), pp. 129–36; Martin Feldstein, "The Economics of the New Unemployment," *The Public Interest* (fall 1973); Andrew Brimmer, *Minimum Wage Proposals, Labor Costs, and Employment Opportunities in the Nation's Capitol* (Brimmer & Co., Inc., 1978), demonstrates the adverse employment

and business migration effects of the minimum wage law in Washington, D.C.

5. Jacob Mincer, "Unemployment Effects of Minimum Wages," *Journal of Political Economy* (August 1976), pp. 87–105.

6. *The Fairmont Papers,* ed. Monroe H. Brown (San Francisco: Institute for Contemporary Studies, 1981), p. 50.

7. Census data reveal a remarkable closing of the educational gap, measured in median years of education, between blacks and whites. In fact the difference is negligible with median years for blacks 12.2 and whites 12.5. However, possession of a high school diploma is not synonymous with the ability to read, write and perform simple numerical calculations. The Coleman Report said that blacks at grade 12 lagged three to five years behind whites on academic achievement.

8. G.M.E. Leistner and W.J. Breytenbach, *The Black Worker of South Africa* (Pretoria, South Africa: The African Institute, 1975), p. 28.

9. Ibid., p. 28. Rate-for-the-job is the same as our equal-pay-for-equal-work laws.

10. See Armen A. Alchian and Reuben A. Kessel, "Competition, Monopoly, and the Pursuit of Pecuniary Gains," in H. Gregg Lewis, ed., *Aspects of Labor Economics,* fall, (Princeton: University Press, 1962).

11. The federal minimum wage is only one among many minimum wages. Union collective bargaining agreements, the Davis-Bacon Act and others have the economic effect of minimum wages.

12. The assumption here is that the purchasers of the firm's final product do not care whether the product was produced by white or black workers.

13. The assumption here is that people are legally free to enter the market and there are many firms, such as the case of domestic workers, car washers and manufacturing operatives.

14. See U.S. Bureau of the Census, *Negro Population,* 1790–1950 (Washington, D.C., 1918), pp. 166, 503–504.

15. The *New York Times,* Nov. 28, 1972. In the United States, "liberals" are virtually unanimous in their condemnation of South African policy; yet they and black political leaders support some of the same labor policies and union practices that are supported in South Africa in order to handicap blacks. Interestingly enough,

it is U.S. "conservatives" who reject, for the U.S., South African labor and union policy.

16. The effectiveness of the wage demand also depends upon the elasticity of the substitution of capital for labor, i.e., the extent to which machines can be substituted for labor.

17. Union support for these programs may explain why minorities and their political leaders give unions strong political support. Union support for these programs gives the impression that unions are pro-minority. Thus, in an important sense, minorities are captured union constituents. If they do not politically support union goals that put them out of work in the first place, unions will not support the government handouts minorities receive as a result of being out of work.

18. John F. Kennedy, "New England and the South: the Struggle for Industry," *Atlantic Monthly,* January 1954, p. 33.

19. *Congressional Record,* May 25, 1966, p. 11383.

CHAPTER 4

1. Richard B. Freeman, *Black Elite* (New York: McGraw-Hill, 1976), ch. 4, especially pp. 98–99, 107. See also Thomas Sowell, "Three Black Histories," *Essays and Data on American Ethnic Groups* (Washington, D.C.: The Urban Institute, 1978), pp. 7–48, and Thomas Sowell, "Affirmative Action Reconsidered," *The Public Interest* (winter 1976), pp. 47–65.

2. Kenneth J. Arrow, "Models of Job Discrimination," in Anthony Pascal (ed.), *Racial Discrimination in Economic Life* (Boston: D.C. Heath & Co., 1972), pp. 85–86.

3. Finis Welch, "Labor-Market Discrimination: An Interpretation of Income Differences in the Rural South," *Journal of Political Economy* (June 1967), p. 226.

4. See Richard B. Freeman, "Decline of Labor Market Discrimination and Economic Analysis," *American Economic Review* (May 1973), p. 281, table 1.

5. Ibid.

6. Welch, op. cit., p. 235. Welch's study finds that the coefficient of discrimination against black labor is .19 and that against black education is .72.

7. These findings are even more interesting in light of the fact

that black and white female professionals work nearly identical number of weeks per year (47.2 and 46.6 weeks respectively). Further, 42.5 percent of black female professionals and 42 percent of white female professionals work 50 to 52 weeks per year. See U.S. *Census of Population,* 1970: Occupational Characteristics.

8. The Kendall Coefficient (tau) is a widely used measure of the degree of association or correlation between two sets of data.

9. According to the *1970 Census of Population,* vol. 1, 73.5 percent of the U.S. population lives in urban areas and 26.5 percent are rural. The white population that is urban is 72.4 percent. But the black urban population is 81.3 percent. The differences are very striking when comparisons are made on the basis of "central city" versus other areas. For all Americans, 31.5 percent live in central cities. Nearly 28 percent of the white population lives in central cities while 56.9 percent of the black population resides in central cities.

10. See Thomas Sowell, *Ethnic America* (New York: Basic Books, Inc., 1981), pp. 4–13. See also Thomas Sowell, *American Ethnic Groups* (Washington, D.C.: The Urban Institute, 1978), esp., pp. 253–411.

CHAPTER 5

1. There is little distinction to be made between the licensing of occupations and that of businesses. Licensing a taxi regulates the behavior of the driver and licensing a cafe regulates the cafe keeper.

2. This is very important and bears an example. A truck driver can run over a man. The truck driver may have done it accidentally or intentionally. But its being done either way has *nothing* to do with the *effects* of the wheels going over the human body.

3. About three-fourths of all licensing boards are composed solely of practitioners in the occupations that the boards control. See *Occupational Licensing and the Supply of Non-Professional Labor,* Manpower Monograph No. 11 (Washington, D.C.: U.S. Department of Labor, 1969).

4. See Lee Benham, "Demand for Occupational Licensure," in *Occupational Licensure and Regulations,* Simon Rottenburg, ed. (Washington, D.C.: American Enterprise Institute, 1980), pp. 13–25.

5. For a more complete discussion of these and other effects of licensing see Simon Rottenberg, "Economics of Occupational Licensing," in *Aspects of Labor Economics,* A Report of the National Bureau of Economic Research (Princeton, N.J.: Princeton University Press, 1962), pp. 3–20.

6. Stuart Dorsey, "The Occupational Licensing Queue," unpublished manuscript, Center for the Study of American Business, Washington University, St. Louis, Mo.

CHAPTER 6

1. Jitney service differs from taxis in that it picks up passengers who originate at one or more places along a fixed or semi-fixed route. Jitney service, before outlawed, was a very common mode of travel in the U.S. It remains a common form of travel in many countries, particularly those of the Far East and Latin America. The only surviving jitney service in the U.S. is in Atlantic City, N.J., along one major street.

2. These cities are Washington, D.C., Atlanta, Georgia, and Honolulu, Hawaii. Atlanta has recently (1981) enacted an ordinance to restrict the number of taxis.

3. New York City Administrative Code, para. 436-2.0 (Supp. 1969).

4. For all of 1978 and the first six months of 1979, the price for an independent medallion has fluctuated between $50,000 and $60,000. The lower price for a fleet medallion suggests that fleet operation is less profitable than independent operation. Driver theft is a significant problem.

5. Conversation with Sam Pesce, loan officer of the Chase Manhattan Bank in New York City. Mr. Pesce points out that this is the maximum loan for either independent or fleet medallions.

6. Technically, the license price can be approximated by $\sum_{i=1}^{n} \frac{R_i^r - R_i^o}{(1 + r)^i}$ where the superscripts r and o are the receipts in a restricted and open market respectively. Thus, $R^r - R^o$ is the difference in receipts accruing from a protected market. The denominator is the interest rate that yields the present value.

7. Charles Vidich, *The New York Cab Driver and His Fare* (Cambridge, Mass.: Schenkman Publishing Co., 1976), p. 135.

8. See *New York Times,* "The Taxicab Mess," July 27, 1969, p. 46, col. 1.

9. Michael J. Lazar, "The Non-Medallioned Industry: A Transportation Phenomena," Nov. 19, 1971, *City Record Supplement.*

10. See *New York Times* (Jan. 13, 1969), Section C, p. 21. "Ignore them and you may be putting yourself in the care of a murderer, a thief, or even a rapist. The gypsy driver, by the very fact that he solicits on the street, is at least a crook, but he may have big ideas which include you."

11. Charles Vidich, op. cit., p. 148.

12. Ibid., p. 146.

13. Pennsylvania Public Utilities Commission, *Bus and Taxicab Regulations,* as adopted April 15, 1946, with amendments thereto, Harrisburg, Pa., Apr. 1, 1967.

14. *Philadelphia Inquirer,* May 28, 1979, p. 8A.

15. See *Philadelphia Inquirer,* May 27, 1979, p. 18A.

16. This information was obtained from Public Utility Commission, Office of Enforcement, files in Harrisburg, Pa., Apr. 19, 1979.

17. See, District of Columbia Register, Special Edition, D.C. Rules and Regulations, Title 14 (Washington, D.C.: Public Service Commission, Jan. 10, 1975), p. 71. The relevant passages are in the appendix to this chapter, pp. 87–88.

18. See Hearings before the Subcommittee on Public Utilities, Insurance, and Banking of the Committee on the District of Columbia, House, 85th Cong.: Taxicab Industry in the District of Columbia (Washington, D.C.: Government Printing Office, June 24–26, July 3, 8, 9, 10, 12, 18, 23, 24, 1957), p. 425.

19. U.S. Congress, House, Committee on the District of Columbia, *Taxicab Regulation Staff Report* (Washington, D.C.: Government Printing Office, 1976), p. 281.

20. Ibid., pp. 278–296.

21. Telephone conversations with Malcolm Wood and Mrs. Hill of the District Public Service Commission.

22. Clearly, incumbent black taxi owners in Washington, D.C., would benefit from market closures. In this sense they do not differ from whites as beneficiaries of closed entry.

23. Martin Wohl, "The Taxi's Role in Urban America: Today and Tomorrow," *Transportation,* 1975, pp. 155–56.

CHAPTER 7

1. Until the Court stopped it in 1951, to become a master plumber in Illinois took longer than it took to become a Fellow of the American College of Surgeons. See Walter Gellhorn, "The Abuse of Occupational Licensing," *Chicago Law Review* (fall 1976).

2. 42 Washington, 237, 84 Pacific 851 (1906).

3. *People* v. *Warden,* 144 New York, 529, 39 N.W. 686 (1895).

4. See Homer Clark, "Occupational Licensing in the Building Industry," *Washington University Law Quarterly* (December 1952), pp. 484–541.

5. Lorenzo Greene and Carter G. Woodson, *The Negro Wage Earner* (Washington, D.C.: The Association for the Study of Negro Life and History, Inc., 1930), p. 192.

6. Sterling D. Spero and Abram L. Harris, *The Black Worker: The Negro and the Labor Movement* (New York: Kennikat Press, Inc., 1931), pp. 477–78.

7. Ibid., pp. 478–79.

8. Ibid., p. 480.

9. Ibid., p. 481.

10. Greene and Woodson, op. cit., p. 320 ff.

11. Ibid., p. 320.

12. Spero and Harris, op. cit., p. 68.

13. Isaac Weld, *Travels Through the States of North America and the Providences of Upper and Lower Canada* (London: J. Stockdale, 1799), vol. I, pp. 145–52.

14. James Weldon Johnson, *Along This Way* (New York: Viking, 1937), p. 32.

15. Cited in Herbert Hill, "The Racial Practices of Organized Labor," in Arthur M. Ross & Herbert Hill (ed.), *Employment, Race and Poverty* (New York: Harcourt Brace & World, Inc., 1967), p. 375.

16. John Stephen Durham, "The Labor Unions and the Negro," *Atlantic Monthly,* vol. 81 (February 1898), pp. 226.

17. Ibid., p. 226.

18. Ibid., p. 227.

19. Hill, op. cit., p. 378.

20. Ibid., p. 379.

21. Herbert R. Northrup, *Organized Labor and the Negro* (New York: Harper & Bros., 1944), pp. 1–5.

22. Benjamin Shimberg, *et al., Occupational Licensing* (Washington, D.C.: Public Affairs Press, 1973), pp. 112–13.

23. Ibid., p. 113.

24. Ibid., p. 123.

25. Equal Employment Opportunity Commission, news release, May 19, 1970.

26. United States Commission on Civil Rights, *The Challenge Ahead: Equal Opportunity in Referral Unions* (Washington, D.C.: Government Printing Office, May 1976), p. 25.

27. Herbert Hammerman, "Minority Workers in Construction Referral Unions," *Monthly Labor Review,* May 1972.

28. Alex Maurizi, "Occupational Licensing and the Public Interest," *Journal of Political Economy* (March 1974), pp. 399–413.

29. See Thomas G. Moore, "The Purpose of Licensing," *Journal of Law and Economics* (October 1961), pp. 93–117.

30. Sidney L. Carroll and Robert J. Gaston, "Occupational Licensing," an unpublished National Science Foundation Report, August 1977.

31. *Parker* v. *Brown,* 317 U.S. 341, 350–52 (1943).

32. *Griggs* v. *Duke Power Co.,* 401 US 424 (1971).

CHAPTER 8

1. A yellow-dog contract is one in which the employee agrees not to join a union.

2. Herbert R. Northrup, "The Appropriate Bargaining Unit Question Under the Railway Labor Act," *Quarterly Journal of Economics,* vol. 60 (February 1946), p. 254.

3. 137 F2d 817 (D.C. Cir. 1943), rev., 320 U.S. 715 (1943).

4. For additional problems and examples see Howard W. Risher, Jr., *The Negro in the Railroad Industry* (Philadelphia, Pa.: University of Pennsylvania Press, 1971), especially chapters 4–7.

5. 323 U.S. 192, 202–203 (1944).

6. Ibid.

7. Risher, op. cit.

8. U.S. *Census of the Population: 1940,* vol. 3, *The Labor Force,* pt. I, Table 62.

9. Cited by Herbert Hill, "The Racial Practices of Organized Labor," in *Employment, Race and Poverty,* Arthur M. Ross & Herbert Hill, ed. (New York: Harcourt Brace & World, 1967).

10. *Locomotive Firemen's Magazine* (August 1899), p. 203.

11. Despite a general consensus among today's public that people should be paid identically if they do identical work, this law is the first step toward handicapping the most disadvantaged group of workers.

12. Sterling D. Spero and Abram L. Harris, *The Black Worker* (New York: Kennikat Press, 1931), p. 291.

13. Ibid., p. 293.

14. Charles H. Houston, "Foul Employment Practice on the Rails," *Crisis* (October 1949), pp. 269–84.

15. Hill, op cit., p. 389.

16. Ibid., p. 390.

17. Ibid., p. 390.

18. Ibid., pp. 390–91.

CHAPTER 9

1. See Thomas G. Moore, *Freight Transportation Regulation* (Washington, D.C.: American Enterprise Institute, 1972), for an excellent summary of the history of the Interstate Commerce Act and its amendments.

2. Ibid., p. 26.

3. Alfred E. Kahn, *The Economics of Regulation: Principles and Institutions* (New York: John Wiley & Sons, 1971), vol. II, p. 14. See discussion on page 28 on the tendency of regulation to spread.

4. This information was obtained through conversations with various truck sales and banking establishments in the Philadelphia area. There is considerable variation in the prices of trailers since they are specialized in use, but they range from $7,000 to $20,000 depending on intended load.

5–6. See John W. Snow and Stephen Sobotka, "Certificate Values," in *Regulation of Entry and Pricing in Truck Transportation,*

Paul W. MacAvoy and John W. Snow, eds. (Washington, D.C.: American Enterprise Institute, 1977), pp. 153–58. As an example, when the large Associated Transport Company went bankrupt, it sold its certificate of authorization for $20 million.

7. Motor Carrier Code 190, 203.

8. Harold Demsetz, "Why Regulate Utilities?" *Journal of Labor Economics* (April 1968).

9. "Mover's Fight for a National License," *New York Times,* May 4, 1979, p. D1.

10. American Trucking Association, *Accounting for Motor Carrier Operating Rights,* Brief and Petition of American Trucking Association, Inc., before the Financial Standards Board of the Financial Accounting Foundation, Washington, D.C., 1974.

11. Interstate Commerce Commission, Office of Policy and Analysis, *Economic Impact of New Motor Carrier Entry for the Transportation of Government Traffic* (Washington, D.C.: Interstate Commerce Commission, March 1979).

12. Class I carriers are those having annual gross revenues of $3 million or more; Class II carriers are those having gross revenues of $500,000 to $2,999,999; Class III carriers are those having gross revenues less than $500,000. See *Motor Carrier Statistical Summary* (Washington, D.C.: American Trucking Association, Inc., 1977).

13. Asil Gezen and Marion Forrester, TERA, Inc., *A Report on OMBRE's Minority Trucking Program,* (DOC Contract No. 6–11685), p. 16.

14. Government Accounting Office, "Minority Motor Carriers Can Be Given More Opportunity to Participate in Defense Transportation" (Washington, D.C.: General Accounting Office, June 6, 1978).

15. Ibid., p. 11.

16. See statement of Timothy D. Person before the Subcommittee on Special Small Business Problems of the House Committee on Small Business: Regulatory Problems of the Independent Owner-Operator in the Nation's Trucking Industry, Sept. 29, 1977.

17. U.S. Department of Commerce, Bureau of the Census, *1972 Survey of Minority-Owned Business Enterprises,* MB 72–1 (Washington, D.C.: Government Printing Office, November 1974).

18. The category includes freight forwarders, limousine companies, etc.

19. Testimony of Timothy D. Person before Hearings Subcommittee on Activities of Regulatory Agencies of the Committee on Small Business, House, 94th Congress: Regulatory Problems of the Independent Owner-Operator in the Nation's Trucking Industry (Part one), p. 267, May 19, 1976.

20. 353 I.C.C. 425 (1977).

21. Jack Anderson, *Washington Post,* Wednesday, July 26, 1978, p. C27.

22. William B. Gould, *Black Workers in White Unions* (Ithaca: Cornell University Press, 1977).

23. See *Franks* v. *Bowman Transportation Co.,* 495 F 2d 398 (5th Cir.), cert. denied, 419 U.S. 1050 (1974); *U.S.* v. *Navaho Freight Lines, Inc.,* 525 F 2d 1318 (9th Cir. 1975); *Hairston* v. *McLean Trucking Co.,* 520 F 2d 226 (4th Cir. 1975); *U.S.* v. *T.I.M.E.—D.C., Inc.,* 517 F 2d 299 (5th Cir. 1975); *Saba* v. *Western Gillette, Inc.,* 516 F 2d 1251 (5th Cir. 1975); *Rodriguez* v. *East Texas Motor Freight, Inc.,* 505 F 2d 66 (5th Cir. 1974); *Herrara* v. *Yellow Freight Systems, Inc.,* 505 F 2d 66 (5th Cir. 1974; *U.S.* v. *Lee Way Motor Freight, Inc.,* 505 F 2d 69 (5th Cir. 1975); *Bing* v. *Roadway Express, Inc.,* 444 F 2d 687 (5th Cir. 1971); *U.S.* v. *Lee Way Motor Freight, Inc.,* 6 FEP Cases 274 (C.D. Cal. 1973).

24. Gould, op cit., p. 369.

25. See *United States* v. *Pilot Freight Carriers, Inc.,* 6 FEP Cases 280 (M.D., N.C. July 30, 1973) and *United States* v. *Navajo Freight Lines, Inc.,* 6 FEP Cases 274. (C.D. Cal. June 6, 1973).

26. *United States* v. *Lee Way Motor Freight, Inc.,* 6 FEP Cases 274 (C.D. Cal. 1973).

27. "Bias in the Cab," *Wall Street Journal,* Mar. 31, 1966, pp. 1, 6.

28. FEP Cases at 745 and 7 FEP Cases at 729.

29. Many teamsters unions have formal or informal exclusive hiring arrangements with employers of truck drivers which require that the employer hire drivers on a referral basis from the union hall. This permits wide scope for racial discrimination.

30. Article I., Section 8 of the U.S. Constitution gives Congress the power: "To regulate Commerce with foreign Nations, and among the several States, and with the Indian Tribes."

31. *Butcher's Union Co.* v. *Crescent City Co.,* 111 U.S. 746, 762 (1884).

32. *Dent* v. *West Virginia,* 129 U.S. 114, 121 (1888).

33. *Barsky* v. *Board of Regents of New York,* 347 U.S. 442, 472 (1954).

34. Report in *United States Law Week* (Nov. 7, 1978), p. 47.

35. 42 U.S.C. paragraph 6705 (f) (2).

36. The Davis-Bacon Act of 1931, along with its subsequent amendments, requires that "prevailing wages" be paid on all federally financed or assisted construction projects. Considerable consensus among economists shows that the Davis-Bacon Act discriminates against non-union contractors and workers. Most minority contractors and employees in the construction industry are in the non-union sector. For insightful analysis of the Davis-Bacon Act, see General Accounting Office Report to Congress. "The Need for More Realistic Minimum Rate Determinations for Certain Federally Financed Housing in Washington Metropolitan Area" (Washington, D.C.: Government Printing Office, 1968); Richard L. Rowan and Lester Rubin, *Opening the Skilled Construction Trades to Blacks* (Philadelphia: University of Pennsylvania Press, 1972); Yale Brozen, "The Davis-Bacon Act: How to Load the Dice Against Yourself" (unpublished manuscript, University of Chicago, 1971); John P. Gould, *Davis Bacon Act: The Economics of Prevailing Wage Laws* (Washington, D.C.: American Enterprise Institute, 1972); *The Legislative History of the Davis-Bacon Act* (Washington, D.C.: Government Printing Office, 1962); Government Accounting Office Report to the Congress of the United States. *The Davis-Bacon Act Should be Repealed* (Washington, D.C.: Government Printing Office, Apr. 27, 1979).

CHAPTER 10

1. *Munn* v. *Illinois,* 94 U.S. 113 (1877).

2. The relevant portions of the Fifth and Fourteenth amendments respectively are: No person shall . . . be deprived of life, liberty, or property, without due process of law; nor shall private property be taken for public use, without just compensation. Amendment Fourteen, Section 1. All persons born or naturalized in the United States and subject to the jurisdiction thereof, are citizens of the United States and of the State wherein they reside.

No State shall make or enforce any law which shall abridge the privileges or immunities of citizens of the United States; nor shall any State deprive any person of life, liberty, or property, without due process of law; nor deny any person within its jurisdiction the equal protection of the laws.

3. The constitutional safeguard of *substantive due process* requires that all legislation, state or federal, must be reasonably related to the furtherance of a legitimate governmental objective. Not only must the legislation be rationally related, but it must utilize that method of promoting the government interest which is the least burdensome to other rights. *Procedural due process,* on the other hand, guarantees procedural fairness where the government would deprive one of his property or liberty. This requires that notice and the right to a fair hearing be accorded prior to a deprivation. See Steven H. Gifis, *Law Dictionary* (New York: Barron's Educational Series, Inc., 1975), pp. 66–67.

4. *Mugler* v. *Kansas,* 123 U.S. 623 (1887).

5. *Allgeyer* v. *Louisiana,* 165 U.S. 578 (1897).

6. Ibid., 578, 579 (1897).

7. *Lochner* v. *New York,* 198 U.S. 45 (1905).

8. Ibid.

9. Especially interesting cases during this period were: *Nielson* v. *Oregon,* 212 U.S. 315 (1909); *Dozier* v. *Alabama,* 218 U.S. 124 (1910); *Crenshaw* v. *Arkansas,* 227 U.S. 389 (1913); *Adams* v. *Tanner,* 244 U.S. 590 (1917); *Buck* v. *Kuykendall,* 567 U.S. 307 (1925); *Louis K. Liggett Co.* v. *Baldridge,* 278 U.S. 105 (1928).

10. See *Moorehead* v. *New York ex rel. Tipaldo,* 298 U.S. 587 (1936); *New State Ice Co.* v. *Liebman,* 235 U.S. 262 (1932); *Williams* v. *Standard Oil Co.,* 278 U.S. 235 (1929); *Ribnick* v. *McBride,* 277 U.S. 350 (1928); *Tyson & Brother* v. *Banton,* 273 U.S. 418 (1927); *Adkins* v. *Children's Hospital,* 261 U.S. 525 (1923); *Adams* v. *Turner,* 244 U.S. 590 (1917); *Coppage* v. *Kansas,* 236 U.S. 1 (1915); *Adair* v. *United States,* 208 U.S. 161 (1908); *Lochner* v. *New York,* 198 U.S. 45 (1905).

11. *New State Ice Co.* v. *Liebman,* op. cit.

12. Ibid.

13. *Nebbia* v. *New York,* 291 U.S. 502 (1934).

14. Ibid., 502, 525 (1934).

15. Ibid., 502, 554–55 (1934).

16. *West Coast Hotel Co.* v. *Parrish,* 300 U.S. 379 (1937).

17. *Adkins* v. *Children's Hospital,* op. cit.

18. *National Labor Relations Board* v. *Jones & Laughlin Steel,* 301 U.S. 1.

19. *Adair* v. *United States,* 208 U.S. 161 (1908).

20. *Coppage* v. *Kansas,* op. cit. 236 U.S. (1915).

21. 300 U.S. 379 (1937).

22. 304 U.S. 144 (1938).

23. 313 U.S. 236 (1941).

24. 313 U.S. 246 (1941).

25–26. 342 U.S. 421 (1952).

27. 342 U.S. 423 (1952).

28. 348 U.S. 487 (1955).

29. See Robert G. McCloskey, "Economic Due Process and the Supreme Court: An Exhumation and Reburial," Philip B. Kurland, ed., *The Supreme Court Review* (1962), pp. 42–43.

30. *Tyson & Brother* v. *Banton,* 273 U.S. 446 (1927), dissenting opinion.

31. *Barsky* v. *Board of Regents of New York,* 347 U.S. 472 (1954), dissenting opinion.

32. *Allgeyer* v. *Louisiana,* op. cit., 578, 589 (1897).

33. *Butcher's Union Co.* v. *Crescent City Co.,* 111 U.S. 746, 762 (1884), concurring opinion.

34. *Dent* v. *West Virginia,* 129 U.S. 114, 121 (1888).

35. *Williamson* v. *Lee Optical Company of Oklahoma,* 348 U.S. 483, 487, 488 (1955).

36. *Day-Brite Lighting* v. *Missouri,* 342 U.S. 421, 423 (1952).

37. *Ferguson* v. *Skrupa,* 372 U.S. 730, 732 (1963). Contrast this attitude of the Court, particularly that of Douglas, with that held in most civil rights cases. That is, the Court *did* substitute its judgment for that of the state legislatures on civil rights issues.

38. 347 U.S. 442 (1954).

39. See Robert G. McCloskey, "Economic Due Process and the Supreme Court: An Exhumation and Reburial," *The Supreme Court Review* (1962), pp. 26, 27.

40. 353 U.S. 232 (1957).

41. Ibid.

42. 353 U.S. 239 (1957).

43. Ibid.

44. *Griggs* v. *Duke Power Company,* 401 U.S. 424 (1971).

CHAPTER 11

1. Milton Friedman, *Capitalism and Freedom* (Chicago: University of Chicago Press, 1962), p. 92.

2. For a more thorough examination of these principles see Harold Demsetz, "Minorities in the Market Place," *North Carolina Law Review* (February 1965), pp. 271–99; Alchian and Kessel, "Competition, Monopoly, and the Pursuit of Pecuniary Gain," in *Aspects of Labor Economics* (National Bureau of Economic Research, 1962).

BIBLIOGRAPHY

Barber, Thomas H., *Where We Are At.* New York: Charles Scribner's Sons, 1950.

Barger, Melvin D., "Occupational Licensing Under Attack," in *Freeman,* April 1975.

Bauer, P.T., *West African Trade: A Study of Competition, Oligopoly and Monopoly in a Changing Economy.* New York: Augustus M. Kelley Publishers, 1954.

Blaisdell, Ruth F., *et al.* compilers, *Sources of Information in Transportation.* Evanston, Ill.: Northwestern University Press, 1964.

Blalock, Hubert M. Jr., *Toward a Theory of Minority Group Relations.* New York: Wiley, 1967.

Bland, Randall W., *Constitutional Law in the United States.* Florida: Omni Press, Inc., 1976.

Bradley, Philip D. (ed.), *The Public Stake in Union Power.* Charlottesville: University of Virginia Press, 1959.

Chamberlain, Edward H., Philip D. Bradley, Gerald D. Reilly, Roscoe Pound, *Labor Unions and Public Policy.* Washington, D.C.: American Enterprise Institute, 1958.

Clark, Homer S., "Occupational Licensing in the Building Industry," in *Washington University Law Quarterly,* December 1952.

Conant, Michael, *The Constitution and Capitalism.* St. Paul, Minn.: West Publishing Co., 1974.

Davidson, Roger H., and Sar A. Levitan, *Anti-Poverty Housekeeping: The Administration of the Economic Opportunity Act.* Michigan: The Institute of Labor and Industrial Relations, 1968.

Dorsey, Stuart, "Characteristics of the Occupational Licensing Queue," unpublished paper, Western Illinois University.

Du Bois, W.E.B., *The Philadelphia Negro* (1899).

_____, (ed.), *The Negro Artisan* (Atlanta, 1902).

_____, "The Economic Future of the Negro," *American Economic Association Publications* (1906).

_____, "The Passing of Jim Crow," *The Independent,* July 14, 1917, pp. 53–54.

_____, "The Host of Black Labor," *The Nation,* May 9, 1923, pp. 539–41.

Eckert, Ross D., *Regulatory Commission Behavior: Taxi Franchising in Los Angeles and Other Cities.* University of California, Los Angeles, Ph.D. dissertation, 1968.

_____, "The Los Angeles Taxicab Monopoly: An Economic Inquiry," in *Southern California Law Review,* vol. 45, summer 1970.

Eckert, Ross D., and George W. Hilton, "The Jitneys," *Journal of Law and Economics,* vol. 15 (October 1972), pp. 293–327.

Fitzhugh, George, "What's to Be Done with the Negroes?" *DeBow's Review.* New Series I (June 1866): 577–81.

Foner, Philip S., and Ronald L. Lewis (eds.), *The Black Worker to 1869.* Philadelphia: Temple University Press, 1978, vol. I.

_____, *The Black Worker During the Era of the National Labor Union.* Philadelphia: Temple University Press, 1978.

Friedman, Lawrence, "Freedom of Contract and Occupational Licensing 1890–1910: A Legal and Social Study," in *California Law Review,* vol. 53, 1965.

Friedman, Milton, *Capitalism and Freedom.* Chicago: University of Chicago Press, 1962.

Garfield, Paul J., and Wallace F. Lovejoy, *Public Utility Economics.* Englewood Cliffs, N.J.: Prentice-Hall, Inc., 1964.

Gellhorn, Walter, *Individual Freedom and Government Restraints.* Baton Rouge: Louisiana University Press, 1956.

_____, "Abuse of Occupational Licensing," in *University of Chicago Law Review,* vol. 44, fall 1976.

Gould, William B., *Black Workers in White Unions: Job Discrimination in the United States.* Ithaca, N.Y.: Cornell University Press, 1977.

Greene, Lorenzo J., and Carter G. Woodson, *The Negro Wage Earner.* New York: Van Rees Press, 1930.

Greene, Lorenzo J., *The Negro in Colonial New England.* New York: Atheneum, 1969.

Gross, James A., "Historians and the Literature of the Negro Worker," *Labor History* (1969).

Harris, Abram L., *The Negro as Capitalist.* Philadelphia: American Academy of Political and Social Science, 1936.

Higgs, Robert, *Competition and Coercion: Blacks in the American Economy, 1865–1914.* New York: Cambridge University Press, 1977.

Huggins, Nathan I., Martin Kilson, and Daniel M. Fox; under the general editorship of John Morton Blum, *Key Issues in the Afro-American Experience.* New York: Harcourt Brace Jovanovich, 1971.

Hutt, William H., *The Economics of the Color Bar.* London: The Institute of Economic Affairs, Ltd., 1964.

————, *The Strike-Threat System.* New York: Arlington House, 1973.

Johnson, Charles, "Negro Workers in the Unions," *Survey* (Apr. 15, 1928), pp. 113–15.

Johnson, Thomas H., *The Oxford Companion to American History.* New York: Oxford University Press, 1966.

Kain, John F., and John R. Meyer (eds.), *Essays in Regional Economics,* 1971.

Kennedy, Louise Venable, *The Negro Peasant Turns Cityward.* New York: AMS Press, Inc., 1968.

Kitch, Edmund W., Mark Isaacson and Daniel Kasper, "The Regulation of Taxicabs in Chicago," *The Journal of Law and Economics* (October 1971), vol. XIV, pp. 285–350.

Kitch, Edmund W., "The Yellow Cab Anti-trust Case," *The Journal of Law and Economics,* vol. 15 (October 1972), pp. 327–36.

Litwack, Leon F., *North of Slavery: The Negro in the Free States, 1790–1860.* Chicago: University of Chicago Press, 1961.

Logan, Rayford W., *The Negro in American Life and Thought.* New York: Dial Press, Inc., 1954.

————, *The Betrayal of the Negro, from Rutherford B. Hayes to Woodrow Wilson.* New York: Collier Books, 1965.

Manpower Research Monograph, U.S. Department of Labor, Manpower Administration.

Marshall, F. Ray, "Union Racial Practices," statement before the U.S. Senate Subcommittee on Labor and Public Welfare, Hearing, 88th Congress, Aug. 6–7 and Sept. 10, 11, 13, 1963.

Maurizi, Alex, "Occupational Licensing and the Public Interest," in *Journal of Political Economy,* March–April 1974.

McCloskey, Robert G., "Economic Due Process and the Supreme Court: An Exhumation and Reburial," in Philip B. Kurland (ed.), *1962 Supreme Court Review 34.*

McPherson, James M. *et al., Blacks in America.* Garden City, N.Y.: Doubleday, 1971.

Meier, August, and Elliott Rudwic, *From Plantation to Ghetto.* New York: Hill and Wang, 1970.

Miller, W. Elizabeth, and Mary L. Fisher, *The Negro in America.* Cambridge: Harvard University Press, 1970.

Moore, Thomas G., "The Purpose of Licensing," in *Journal of Law and Economics,* October 1961.

———, *Freight Transportation Regulation, Surface Freight and Interstate Commerce Commission.* Washington, D.C.: American Enterprise Institute for Public Policy Research, 1972.

———, "The Beneficiaries of Trucking Regulation," *The Journal of Law and Economics* (October 1978), vol. 21 (2), pp. 327–42.

Muller, Helen M., *Federal Regulation of Motor Transport.* New York: The Wilson Co., 1933. Part of "The Reference Shelf" series, vol. VIII, no. 9.

Myrdal, Gunnar, *An American Dilemma.* New York: Harper, 1944.

National Bureau of Economic Research, *Aspects of Labor Economics.* Princeton, N.J.: Princeton University Press, 1962.

Oak, Vishnu V., *The Negro's Adventure in General Business.* Westport, Conn.: Negro University Press, 1949.

Occupational Licensing and the Supply of Non-Professional Labor. Washington, D.C.: Department of Labor, 1969. Manpower monograph No. 11.

Oi, Walter Y., *Economics of Private Truck Transportation.* Dubuque, Iowa: William C. Brown Company, Publisher, 1965.

Okon Edet Uya, *From Slavery to Public Service: Robert Smalls 1839–1915.* New York: Oxford University Press, 1971.

Perlman, Selig, *A Theory of the Labor Movement.* New York: Augustus M. Kelley, Publisher, 1966.

Pejovich, Svetozar, and David Klingaman, *Individual Freedom: Selective Works of William H. Hutt.* London: Greenwood Press, 1975.

Pejovich, Svetozar (ed.), *Governmental Controls and the Free Market: The U.S. Economy in the 1970's.* College Station: Texas A&M University Press, 1976.

Pfeffer, J., "Some Evidence on Occupational Licensing and Occupational Income," in *Social Forces,* vol. 53, September 1974.

Price, Daniel O., *Changing Characteristics of the Negro Population.* Washington, D.C.: Government Printing Office, 1969. A 1960 Census monograph.

Reid, Ira De A., *Negro Membership in American Labor Unions.* New York: The Alexander Press, 1930.

――――, *The Negro Immigrant: His Background, Characteristics and Social Adjustment, 1899–1937.* New York: AMS Press, 1970.

Renshaw, Patrick, "The Black Ghetto, 1890–1940," *Journal of American Studies,* 1974.

Risher, Howard W., *The Negro in the Railroad Industry.* Philadelphia: University of Pennsylvania Press, 1971. The Racial Policies of American Industry, Report No. 16, with assistance of Marjorie C. Denison.

Roche, John P., *Sentenced to Life.* New York: Macmillan Publishing Co., Inc., 1974.

Rosenbloom, Sandi, "Taxis and Jitneys: The Case for Deregulation," *Reason* (February 1972), pp. 4–16.

Rottenberg, Simon, "The Economics of Occupational Licensing," in *Aspects of Labor Economics,* Princeton, N.J.: National Bureau of Economic Research, Princeton University Press, 1962.

Schubert, Gledon A., *Constitutional Politics.* New York: Holt, Rinehart & Winston, Inc., 1960.

Scott, Emmett J., *Negro Migration During the War.* New York: Oxford University Press, 1920.

Shimberg, Benjamin, Barbara F. Esser, and Daniel H. Kruger, *Occupational Licensing: Practices & Policies.* Washington, D.C.: Public Affairs Press, 1972.

――――, *Improving Occupational Regulation.* Princeton, N.J.: Educational Testing Service, 1976.

Siverman, Irwin W., L. T. Bennett, and Irvin Lechliter, "Control by Licensing over Entry into the Market," *Law and Contemporary Problems,* spring 1941.

Spero, Sterling D. and Abram L. Harris, *The Black Worker: The Negro and the Labor Movement.* New York: Kennikat Press, Inc., 1931.

Starobin, Roberts, *Industrial Slavery in the Old South.* New York: Oxford University Press, 1970.

Stiglitz, Joseph, "Approaches to the Economics of Discrimination," *American Economic Review* 63 (May 1973), 287–95.

Stern, Robert L., "The Problems of Yesteryear—Commerce and Due Process," *Vanderbilt Law Review* (4/51), pp. 446–68.

Stone, Alfred Holt, *Studies in the American Race Problems,* New York: Doubleday Page and Co., 1908.

"The Negro in Unskilled Labor," *Annals of the American Academy of Political and Social Science 49,* September 1913, pp. 19–27.

Thirsk, Joan, and J.P. Cooper (eds.), *Seventeenth-Century Economic Documents.* London: Oxford University Press, 1972.

U.S. Bureau of the Census, Sixteenth (1940) *Population: Comparative Occupational Statistics for U.S. 1870–1940,* Washington, D.C., 1943.

U.S. Bureau of the Census, *Historical Statistics of the U.S.* U.S. Government Printing Office, 2nd edition, 1960.

U.S. Department of Labor, "Conditions of the Negro in Various Cities," Bulletin # 10, pp. 257–69 (1897).

Virkuil, Paul R., "The Economic Regulation of Taxicabs," *Rutgers Law Review,* vol. 24 (1970), pp. 673–711.

Wagner, Warren H., *A Legislative History of the Motor Carrier Act.* Denton, Md.: RUE Publishing Co., 1935.

Washington, Booker T., *Up from Slavery: An Autobiography.* London: Oxford University Press, 1945 (1901).

———, "The Negro and the Labor Unions," *Atlantic Monthly* 111, June 1913: 756–67.

Welch, Finis, "Labor-Market Discrimination: An Interpretation of Income Differences in the Rural South: *Journal of Political Economy* 75 (June 1967): 225–40.

Wesley, Charles H., *Negro Labor in the United States—1850–1925.* New York: Russell & Russell, 1967.

Wharton, Vernon Lane, *The Negro in Mississippi, 1865–90.* University of North Carolina Press, 1947.

White, D.M., and R.L. Francis, "Title VII and the Masters of Reality: Eliminating Credentialism in the American Labor Market," in *Georgetown Law Journal,* July 1976.

Wiprud, Arne C., *Justice in Transportation: An Exposé of Monopoly Control.* New York: Ziff-Davis Publishing Co., 1945.

Wisconsin Legislative Council Staff, "Regulation and Licensing: An Overview," *Research Bulletin No. 76-7,* Madison, Wis., July 1976.

Wollett, Donald H., and Benjamin Arron, *Labor Relations and the Law.* Boston: Little, Brown & Co., 1960.

Worthman, Paul B., "Black Workers and Labor Unions in Birmingham, Alabama—1897-1904," *Labor History,* 1969.

Wyckoff, Daryl D., and David H. Maister, *The Owner-Operator: Independent Trucker.* Lexington, Mass.: D.C. Heath & Co., 1975.

————, *The Motor Carrier Industry.* Lexington, Mass.: D.C. Heath & Co., 1977.

INDEX